A GARDEN EDEN IN NORTHERN REVISITED MOROCCO

UMBERTO PASTI &
NGOC MINH NGO

FOREWORD BY
MARTINA MONDADORI

New York · Paris · London · Milan

FOR THE CHILDREN OF ROHUNA

CONTENTS

- 6   FOREWORD
- 10   ENTERING EDEN
- 16   THE GARDEN OF CONSOLATION
  - 20   *Lotfi's Garden*
  - 38   *The Winter House*
  - 52   *Nabil's Garden*
  - 70   *The Garden of the Portuguese*
  - 78   *The Bone Garden*
  - 86   *The Garden of the Englishman*
  - 96   *The Exedra Under the Fig Tree*
  - 104   *The Rotunda*
  - 112   *The Summer House*
  - 118   *The Wild Room*
  - 122   *Stephan's Terrace*
  - 128   *Chinioui's Terraces*
  - 148   *The Garden of the Italian*
  - 160   *Hamidou's Garden*
- 176   THE WILD GARDEN
- 186   THE GHARSA BAQQALI
- 208   WILD FLOWERS OF NORTHERN MOROCCO
- 226   THE TRUE GARDEN
- 234   PLANT LIST

FOREWORD

MARTINA MONDADORI

My father, Leonardo Mondadori, had a passion for gardens. From my earliest childhood I visited many — in England, Italy, France, and the United States. But it is only thanks to Umberto Pasti that in these last few years I have begun to appreciate and love gardens. Everything began with my first visit to Rohuna a few years ago. I realized I had never seen anything like it.

It is a magnificent landscape, bare and harsh. The garden opens up in front of you like the sweetest of oases. And yet, as soon as you enter, you become lost in its small walkways and paths that cross the open-air rooms and emerge in flowery meadows. Strange as it may seem, this garden is a condensation of its landscape, a distillation of the countryside. It captures the spirit of the northern Morocco that Umberto loves so deeply; it is the essence of this love. And being in Rohuna with him is like being inside this love. I am especially fond of the rooms of this garden, opening up before you one after the other. Even the few pieces of furniture that Umberto has arranged in them were born here, being made of arbutus wood by local craftsmen whom Umberto has affectionately trained since their childhood.

My happiness must also come from the thought of the countless plants and wild flowers that Umberto and his young gardeners have rescued from the development sites that are destroying this corner of the world. Or perhaps it has something to do with his close relationship with the *jennun*, the *genii loci*, the spirits of this ancient land. Sure enough, every visit to Rohuna (after the first time I came back as soon as I could) is an unforgettable experience. And thanks to Rohuna, Umberto and I have become even better friends. He is now helping me to create a garden in Tuscany. I would love it to be an Italian Rohuna — the wild flowers, the animals, the children playing, and lovely dinners underneath the pergolas; may its same rural magic charm bring all readers, contributors, and inspirators of my design magazine *Cabana* together into one big happy family.

Umberto has written a number of books. His novel *Perduto in Paradiso*, which tells of his arrival on this bleak coast, of his encounter with its villagers who had never come into contact with a foreigner before, and of the birth of this garden, is a fascinating and moving work. Yet I am sure that this garden itself is his most beautiful book. Rohuna is his masterpiece. It reflects not only his love of beauty in every form, but also his love of freedom — in thought and in life — that makes him an extraordinary human being.

It is a blessing for us all that Umberto's and Ngoc's paths crossed. In her wonderful photographs Ngoc has succeeded in capturing the spirit of this garden, season after season, and she has done so with great depth of sensitivity, hard work, and impeccable technique. Entering this garden of the Hesperides, which is located right after the pillars of Hercules, you will come to understand why Rohuna is so very reminiscent of Eden.

ENTERING EDEN

Rohuna is a village of some five hundred people on the Atlantic coast of northern Morocco; it lies forty miles south of Tangier between the towns of Asilah and Larache. I arrived twenty years ago with a friend who lived here and who wanted to show me a place where no *nazrani*, no foreigner, had ever set foot before. I was curious and a little skeptical — I had been living in Tangier for quite a while, and had extensively explored the region.

The path came out in a space paved with large whitewashed stones. There was a spring. The children watched me with curiosity. A young man greeted us with a nod, hiding his surprise behind the mask of manly indifference. Wrapped in *mendil* like Navajo Indians in their striped blankets, the women averted their eyes. After passing through the village (stone houses with tin roofs, separated by fences of prickly pears) we climbed the hill to the top. The ocean glimmered. We stood on a stony slope overlooking the valley of Eden — empty, innocent, with a river twisting through it. Us and two Bonelli's eagles in flight, and no one else. The first morning of the world.

We came down. There was a fig tree. I sat down in its shade and fell asleep. I dreamt that this place was my body and my body was a garden.

When I woke up I was flowerbeds and stairs and terraces. There was turf where my hair had been. I had turned into a garden that had already been there once, who knows when. Around us there were dry thistles that looked like voodoo pins torturing the earth, tufts of dwarf palms, stones, a few wild olive trees, a few mastic trees with leaves reddened from thirst, and sand dunes down below. I had no time to lose. I told my friend I was going to stay and live here. He cast me a worried glance. I still did not know that the *jennun*, the rural spirits, take hold of those who sleep beneath trees. Dearest *jennun*, who since that distant day have lived within me, have sheltered and guided me! A boy appeared from behind a bush. He was called Rachid. In a few hours he'd built a hut made of reeds and covered with palm leaves (a palm tree grew far down in the valley). That first night we all slept in there. Some days later I called Stephan: "We are moving to the country." He did not seem surprised — he doesn't always take me seriously. But the building project had started. It was a good thing I had recently inherited from my father.

Within a few weeks, I bought the land where in the meantime I had already settled: two acres of stony ground in which two eucalyptus trees grew and an orange tree and two fig trees survived. I had six hundred people working for me, practically all the people of the area. Stephan called it my "Cleopatra syndrome." Tons of rich topsoil arrived on the backs of mules while workers built miles of drystone walls to prevent erosion. From time to time I left the work site and wandered around, trekking among these isolated coastal villages. I paid no attention to the centaurs that appeared from behind boulders covered with lichen; I resisted the sirens who stuck out their tongues at me at the other end of the inverted telescope of the low tide. I gauged the architectural details of the oldest buildings — I had decided to build two houses, and they had to look as if they had been there forever.

The garden was rising, and rising again. It was a time both exciting and exhausting. I was determined to hire only local foremen and masons. No engines, everything had to be done by hand. My workers were shepherd kings and young friends of Achilles and Orestes. Yet, with the clanging of

ABOVE: Workers lower into a large hole dug by hands an uprooted olive tree saved from a roadside. **RIGHT:** Nabil's garden and our public shower 19 years ago, with the palm leaf structures to protect from the ocean wind the citrus trees we had just planted — a little North African Mycenae. **LOWER RIGHT:** The Summer House and its garden.

ABOVE: Najim, who today makes furniture in arbutus wood sold all over the world, together with his nephew Chinioui, now a gardener, and his niece, Homeima. They are transporting the materials with which we built a hut at the top of the hill where we played during an entire winter. **LEFT:** The Summer House in the beginning. **LOWER LEFT:** In the foreground of the almost finished Winter House are the gigantic olive trees that we had transported for kilometers on a structure of poles perched on the backs of six mules. **BOTTOM:** The first accomplices of the golden years, without whom the garden wouldn't exist — standing in the front row are Mustafa on the left, Rachid in the center, and Jelel on the right. Behind them are Abdelillah and Mohammed Bando.

PAGES 10–11: At sunset, in Rohuna, we often live in a Poussin painting.

the sledgehammers and picks breaking the stones, the thundering of boulders tumbling to fill up the drains, in the disemboweled earth, in the dust, Eden had turned into an inferno. The unicorns had slinked off. But the houses were coming out of the earth, and little by little the garden was taking shape. The fairy tale had vanished, but the spirits were hatching a new project. As far as I could guess, what they had in mind was a small African Mycenae.

Two events were crucial in the story of the garden. I owe the first to Jawad, a geologist from Tangier, to whom I will be forever grateful. The drilling had already reached three hundred feet when suddenly a river of mud shot out of the borehole and became more and more liquid and transparent. *Tabarak Allah*! We hugged each other laughing and crying. Until then, for four hard years, the only available water had been a tiny spring full of tadpoles and, later, a well that was as miserly as a merchant from Souss. We had dug it following the instructions of Stephan's twelve-year-old cousin who happened to be a diviner. At last, thanks to Jawad, we could water with a pipe (occasionally but abundantly, as you should do in a dry and hot place), and we could cook, and even allow ourselves the bliss of washing up — I did not have to murder my guests anymore when they expressed the wish to take a shower. I also built a public shower in the middle of the garden, where our neighbors are welcome, as well as a fountain at the entrance for families who do not have running water yet.

The second event took place four years ago with the arrival of Bernard, a Belgian gardener who loves and knows plants as only someone who is hiding an inner scar can. He fell in love with Rohuna and came to live here. Through his knowledge and passion he has helped expand the boundaries of Eden and improve conditions for the plants that were already here. Even though he is only a few years younger than Stephan and I, we call him *l'enfant*.

The strong point of our garden is the collection of indigenous plants (especially bulbs), spanning five acres. But in summer almost everything disappears. So I planted the Garden of Consolation: rooms and terraces to be watered in the hot season. It lies between the Summer House (which replaced the first hut with the roof of leaves and is now reserved for guests with young children and for students) and the Winter House, where we live. Here I have trees, shrubs, perennials, and annuals, whose shade and blossoms keep my spirits up even when the *charqui*, the ruthless east wind, blows, and the temperatures reach 105. At first there were just some damask roses, Madonna lilies, bearded irises, canna, lantana hybrids, viburnums, and strawberry trees (*Arbutus unedo*), saved from the building sites of the seaside tourist areas. Bernard added hundreds of species found in nurseries all over the world. Most of those species are completely unknown to me, whose sole gardening teachers have been a bunch of peasant women from northern Morocco. In summer, my tithonias, cosmos, and zinnias are joined by hibiscus, daturas, abutilons, dasylirions, ipomoeas, and unusual species of gardenias. They all can stand this torrid climate and even love it.

Bernard has even created a terrace, the Garden of the Portuguese. It is teeming with exotic beauties: erythrinas, dombeyas, silk floss trees with spiky trunks, thunbergias, schotias, moringas, crotalarias, and fat South African bulbs that disappear in spring beneath a red horde of poppies. According to the secret and as yet unwritten legend that grows with our garden, this spot has been conceived by João, a melancholic Portuguese botanist who retired to this hill in the eighteenth century after many long journeys through Tanzania and Mozambique, Ghana and Guyana, Central and South America. The entire Garden of Consolation is divided into sections named after several characters invented by me (the Garden of the Englishman, of the Egyptian, of the Italian, of the Aissawa) and is protected by a fairy tale. There is the drunken gentleman who after a scandal came here to hide, giving up neither his gin and tonic nor his thirsty crinums. There is the old man from Cairo who smokes his hookah stretched out beneath the palms, enjoying the perfume of *Mirabilis jalapa* — and many others. With these stories I succeeded in captivating my young shepherds and involving them in activities radically alien to them, such as weeding, pruning, transplanting, mulching, watering, and sweeping. "Come to the *Inglisi*," "The *Talian* is dying of thirst," "Didn't you see all the weeds in the *Portuguisi*?" In the Garden of Consolation words like these are heard all day long. Naming a place or a thing is the most effective way to bring them into existence. It was easy for my boys to include the different parts of the garden in their reality. Since they were born, they are accustomed to the thousand names of an extraordinarily rich toponymy that confers upon the least hump, crevice or gully its own impressive coat of arms. (Little by little, I am charting the names in the valley before they are lost, carried away by modernization.) In the early days, in order to remind them to water my useless dahlias, I had to draw them to the flowers by planting peppers and tomatoes there too. Then I realized that if those same dahlias blossomed in a corner with its own name (and its own story, even if invented), they would be watered at the right time. I think this happens because a place that has been named becomes a bit like a person ("Did you see the garden of the Aissawa? It's so happy!" "Dear Gharsa Baqqali! It's so tired, poor thing!"). Around here the winds themselves have identities: the east wind is a young woman who is desperate to make love; the *ghdiga*, the sea wind, is a giant with icy breath. Even the trees — every apricot tree has its states of mind, every plum tree its shifts of mood. The same thing happens with paths that change their minds: it wasn't us who lost our way, but rather the distracted road that got lost and found itself elsewhere. Even time! When we happen to be late, it is because our time grew tired, impatient, or even bad-tempered, and has decided not to coincide with the time of the person with whom we had an appointment, so it has gathered up its things and left. In the veins of my gardeners flows the blood of Berbers, Phoenicians, Carthaginians, Vandals, Bedouins, and Romans. No wonder if in their hearts, under the veil of Islam, there still beats an indomitable animism that makes the life of a foreigner so full of surprises, and so much fun.

Bernard's instructions are invaluable. Mulching with bracken, which he suggested (or even "imposed"), is the most tiresome annual task of all. But the water not evaporating, the moist soil calling the earthworms to the surface, the luxuriance of the plants, pay us back for the weeks spent on the torrid inland, cutting and shredding hundreds of pounds of bracken, and for the endless trips in our old battered Land Rover to transport it here. This year the *Amaryllis belladonna* are rampant Zulu dancers whose heads are crowned with pink flamingo feathers. Though mistrustful at first, Hamidou, Nabil, Lotfi, Chinioui, Hisham, and their helpers were quickly won over by Bernard's competence, by the speed and precision of his trimming, by his ability to recognize seeds and seedlings. They began to admire him. Now they are fond of him. When he goes away to work in some other garden in Morocco or Europe, everyone misses the *Beljiki*, and his return is invariably celebrated with a sumptuous *tajïne* under the fig trees of the Gharsa Baqqali. In winter, when six species of daffodils and three species of irises are in bloom, the *frutteto di Teto*, the orchard up on the hill, is the most beautiful place on earth. The *jennun* rub their hands in satisfaction.

Twenty years have passed, and the garden still rises, again and again; it constantly changes its shape and amazes me. The acres have become twenty-five, and my babbling has turned into a straight language uttered in a clear voice. In the beginning I filled the mules' packsaddles with just a few sacks of bulbs, but now the trailers of tractors driving along the new road are loaded with hundreds of pounds of wild flowers. They have been rescued from the fields just in time, instead of being crushed by the bulldozers of progress or smothered by concrete.

I have already told the story of Rohuna in a novel, *Perduto in Paradiso* (*Lost in Paradise*). It is the story of my arrival here, the encounter of a *nazrani* driven by his demons to create a garden with a group of people from an inaccessible village, without water or electricity, still living in the golden age. But I do have to mention here those first gardeners: Rachid, the boy who popped out from behind the mastic bush; Mohammed Bando, who had a tooth pulled once a month; and Mustafa, always in his fur hat. By now a great many people have become part of the story of the garden. I spend some months of the year far away from them, but each time I come back we gather all here like gypsies around a fire: Sarah, who began coming here as a young girl; Christopher, who is no longer with us, even though his spirit continues to inspire new waterfalls of scillas and streams of oleander; Davide, my alter-ego editor, with whom I revised almost all of my books on these Atlantic terraces; Ngoc, the photographer of trees and flowers who is convinced that the image of an ancient, beloved fig tree is her self-portrait; Younes, the friend who has nobly helped and sustained us in dealing with thorny bureaucratic matters; Sofia, who understands the plants in such an original way; little Gilda who is discovering love in this garden; Najim, who has become an expert carpenter; and so many other neighbors from the village.

After twenty years of trials and tribulations, of defeats not always followed by blissful consolations (but we humble guests can do nothing else but bow to the will of the *jennun*), Stephan and I are happy. Life goes on, as peaceful and industrious as if we were in a medieval monastery. I am proud of the love for plants that grows stronger every day in our young gardeners. In loving those plants, they love their country, its history, its beauty and culture. And no country deserves more love than northern Morocco, disfigured by progress but rich with a mythical past and still as innocent as a kid who starts living his life.

THE GARDEN OF CONSOLATION

Ever since we found abundant water, thanks to Jawad the geologist, we have been able to irrigate the garden between and around the Winter and the Summer House. When the temperature reaches 105, many of the indigenous plants close or curl their leaves to prevent evaporation, or dry up, or disappear completely because of their summer rest. This manifold part of the garden, green and flowery because of watering and consisting of many rooms, keeps our spirits up — hence the name, the Garden of Consolation. We did not plant it to save endangered species. Rather, in the heart of this magnificent and desolate countryside, we were thinking of ourselves, of our needs and pleasures. It is a garden on a human scale. This is why it has another name, a secret one: the Garden of Man.

1. ENTRANCE
2. JELEL'S HOUSE
3. GARAGE
4. BREAD OVEN
5. LOTFI'S GARDEN
6. THE WINTER HOUSE
7. NABIL'S GARDEN
8. THE GARDEN OF THE PORTUGUESE
9. THE WILD GARDEN
10. THE BONE GARDEN
11. THE GARDEN OF THE ENGLISHMAN
12. THE EXEDRA UNDER THE FIG TREE
13. THE ROTUNDA
14. THE SUMMER HOUSE
15. THE WILD ROOM
16. THE GATE TO THE SEA
17. CHINIOUI'S TERRACES
18. THE GARDEN OF THE ITALIAN
19. HAMIDOU'S GARDEN
20. LUXOR
21. NAJIM'S BRIDGE
22. THE GHARSA BAQQALI

PAGES 16–17: Among the jade plants (*Crassula ovata*), the rockroses (*Cistus ladanifer*) and the rosemary, the big gray agave looks like a prehistoric animal.

Lotfi's Garden

The garden tended by Lotfi is the first by the entrance. It's a sandy slope, with a soil rather acid thanks to the leaves of the large mastic trees that have nourished it for centuries. In summer the thick bracken mulch helps to keep the humidity after watering, allowing the plants to bear the heat. When rains start, it is removed to enable the seeds of the wild flowers (mostly poppies) and the bulbs of the small, heavenly scented *Freesia alba* to sprout.

With Bernard, we have planted various exotic breeds here: a pink *Ceiba speciosa* with a trunk that looks like the leg of an elephant, but covered in thorns; a red *Bauhinia galpinii* whose tiny orchids have colors ranging from strawberry to mango flesh; a couple of African tulip trees (*Spathodea campanulata*); various tecoma shrubs (*Tecoma stans, T. capensis, T. castanifolia, T. fulva, T.* x *smithii* — but the genus *Tecoma*, which is so generous yet content with so little, has more than two hundred species, and I would like to try them all); and many other flowers of bold, colorful shades. A small tropical orchard (mango, passion fruit, papaya, and cherimoya trees) is in its first season. We will see how it reacts to the harshness of an Atlantic winter. Beneath the trees we have planted hundreds of *Narcissus elegans* bulbs that were rescued from the building site for the expansion of Tangier airport.

To the east, towards the village, there are rockroses and spurges, including the indigenous *Euphorbia regis-jubae*. To the west, towards the Winter House, many aeoniums, both species and hybrids; some cacti (*Cereus peruvianus, Dasylirion wheeleri, Echinocactus grusonii* — or mother-in-law's cushion); several aloes (*Aloe vera, A. barberae, A. ferox, A. arborescens, A. marlothii, A. chabaudii, A. distans, A. maculata*); and agaves. To avoid the "Texas gas station garden" effect that spoils so many collections of succulents, I have planted them among strawberry trees and rockroses, viburnums and mallows, with lots of bulbs all around.

Lotfi is twenty years old and the youngest of the gardeners. I have known him since he was born. He is Chinioui's brother and the son of Mohammed Bando (one of my first helpers here in Rohuna) and of Rabia, a strong, nice woman. Unlike the rest of his family, he is quite dark-skinned; that is why in the village he is nicknamed *azi*, the "African boy." With his sweet ways, white teeth, long flapping eyelashes, and wide, coal-black eyes, he reminds me of a young man painted by Gauguin. When I watch him work, I find myself no longer in Morocco but rather sailing between warm islands redolent of frangipani, and sometimes I wonder whether this patch of garden has been inspired by the exotic appearance of its gardener.

1. ENTRANCE
2. BREAD OVEN
3. ORCHARD
4. PERGOLA
5. NABIL'S GARDEN
6. THE GARDEN OF THE PORTUGUESE
7. THE ROTUNDA
8. JELEL'S HOUSE
9. GARAGE

PAGES 22–23: The roof of the Winter House seen from above. It's spring and poppies are blooming.

OPPOSITE: Wild carrots, *Daucus carota*, amid the corn; Mexican flame vine, *Pseudogynoxys chenopodioides*, entwined with *Tithonia rotundifolia*; pale pink trumpet vine, *Podranea ricasoliana*, intermingled with the Cape honeysuckle, *Tecomaria capensis*.

PAGE 26: The small path that leads directly from the garage to the Winter House is bordered with wild daisies, red poppies, and hippeastrum.

PAGE 27: A bench in arbutus wood by Najim, a model named "Regency."

PAGE 28: Palms from the Canary Islands and jacarandas soar in a corner where exotic species are mixed with self-seeded plants, like noble ladies hailing from faraway places dancing among a party of drunken peasants.

PAGE 29: The seeds of *Tithonia rotundiflora* 'The Torch' were given to me many years ago by a friend. Its color, along with that of persimmons, is one of my favorite shades of orange — a liquid flame, scorching and frosty at the same time.

OPPOSITE: *Amaryllis belladonna*, looking like ballerinas with thin legs and pink plumage on their heads.

PAGE 32: After a careful pruning, the branches of an old mastic tree, *Pistacia lentiscus*, allow enough sunlight for the *Echium fastuosum* to flower. **PAGE 33:** The high retaining wall located above the Winter House, deliberately left bare except for a cascade of *Delosperma kofleri*. At its feet, wild oleanders, with poppies in spring and zinnias in summer.

PAGES 34–35: A path bordered by buddleias, sages, brooms, and *Melianthus major* leads to an old olive tree saved from a construction site.

OPPOSITE: Top row from left to right: *Podranea ricasoliana*; *Datura metel* 'Double Purple', livid and highly perfumed; *Helianthus annuus* 'Vanilla Ice', a sunflower of the most tender yellow color. Second row: *Tecomaria capensis* 'Apricot'; *Sphaeralcea fendleri*; *Nerine bowdenii*. Bottom row: Another *Datura metel* 'Double White', also fragrant, in a creamy white that is sensual to the point of obscenity, like flesh glimpsed on one's most intimate pallor, epithelium and petal at the same time; *Chrysanthemum carinatum*, commonly known as the painted daisy; the coral red bloom of *Jatropha multifida*.

The Winter House

This is the main house, whose courtyard is built in concrete upon a water tank used for watering. Here, sheltered from the sea winds, we eat, read, chat, and play cards. Growing in the *bermil*, zinc barrels that once contained gasoline, there are some wild oleanders and one night-blooming jasmine (*Cestrum nocturnum*). Outside many Moroccan peasant houses these containers are used as pots, being less expensive and less fragile than earthenware. On a beautiful arbutus wood *étagère* made by Najim, pots of rare bulbs are displayed during the winter, my collection of hippeastrums in spring, and marigolds and zinnias in summer.

To walk into the garden you pass under our triumphal arch: two vertical posts with two shorter posts across them. The whole is covered in three species of jasmine, red Mexican flame vine, roses, and stephanotis — fragrances are important near the house. In a flowerbed I planted a mulberry tree (to provide shade, as is usual in Mediterranean countries), a big *Strelitzia nicolai*, some cannas, some buddleias to attract butterflies, and a few aromatic herbs.

The kitchen has a fireplace and it is the room where we spend the most time. Its floor and walls are covered in old cement tiles that I retrieved from the house of two English friends in Tangier. The house had been bought by a famous Parisian interior decorator who had thrown the tiles away. I sent the truck to the municipal dump, and with that precious rubbish I not only tiled the floors of the kitchen and the two bathrooms, but also two rooms and two bathrooms in my house in Tangier, as well as many other kitchens and bathrooms here in the village. During his first and only visit, the decorator raved about the beauty of the tiles. When I told him where they came from, he turned to stone.

All the beams in the house were surreptitiously recovered when the government replaced the wooden light poles with poles made of cement. From the kitchen beams hang bunches of herbs, baskets for vegetables, and garlands of red onions and garlic. The entrance is next to the kitchen. We almost never use it for coming in or going out — on its walls are hung old tools brought to me by the village children: shovels, picks, spades, wooden pitchforks, scythes and sickles, shearing scissors, carding brushes, tanning knives, and scrapers. I am especially proud of the olive wood shepherd's staffs that hang in a radial pattern above one of the three doors.

In the living room there is another fireplace — in winter Jelel lights it every afternoon at five o'clock. The windows are tiny, as in the rest of the house, for heat insulation purpose. The best of my collections is here on display: toys made by children using mud, or rags, or the fiber of the dwarf palms; nests; whale bones found on the beach; clay containers for sour milk. These treasures are set out on old shelves of painted wood and on the chests where brides of the Jebala people stored their dowries. In a Victorian ornithologist's chest of drawers I keep several smaller objects: Roman bronze nails, tiny balls of resin as translucent as amber, two lizard eggs given to me by Chinioui, rodent nails, some dried beetles, some ancient fragments of export Roman pottery in a style known as Aretine, Neolithic arrowheads, a gold Islamic ring.

From the living room we go to either the two guest rooms or we climb up to the bedroom that Stephan and I share with a family of Eleonora's falcons. For some years now they have been nesting beneath the extension of the roof over

one of our windows. When the eggs open and the parents have to feed the chicks with reptiles and mice, the smell is rather pungent, but that's how life smells. The pieces of furniture in this room are our old iron bed, made in England for the Moroccan market; the bookshelves; and a Spanish desk I bought from a junk shop. I call the desk "Estrellita" because I found the calling card of one Estrella Toledano Benchimol in one of its drawers. It is hard to imagine a name more in the spirit of the old Tangier. The desk Estrellita hums Jewish songs of North Africa. With the chirping of the hungry baby falcons in the background, they are the melodies of a world in which we all lived in harmony with nature. It is an unforgettable experience to wake up to these songs early in the morning. Not even in a cave covered in moss in the depths of a forest of oak and strawberry trees would I feel as happy as I do in this room.

PAGE 39: A corner of the courtyard in front of the house, with furniture by Najim and an oleander grown in an old gasoline barrel.

OPPOSITE: The lamp in the entrance was a neighbor's cage for his pigeons. Hanging above the gilded Regency mirror that came from a junk dealer in Tangier is a whale rib found on the beach. Dolls and tools from the village are arranged on the traditional painted bride chest.

PAGES 42 & 43: All the pieces of furniture in the kitchen were purchased at the markets in the region. The zinc bucket full of sunflowers sits on a painted whale vertebra that was once used as a stool in a house in the village.

PAGES 44 & 45: Two details of the living room. The birds — made of wood, iron, ceramic, and plaster — came from different regions of Morocco. In front of the nineteenth-century Italian desk that ended up in Tangier — who knows how — is a chair by Najim. The Spanish white chairs come from a barber's shop in Asilah. Once upon a time, the ceiling beams were lampposts.

OPPOSITE: Under a whale vertebra, a small painted chest from a shop in Ouezzane. The table came from a dressing room in a *pensione* in Tetouan. The Byzantine gladiolus appears content with the harmony of grays and blues, and smiles.

PAGES 48 & 49: The warrior on horseback is a charming work of the "Straw Zoo," a small association of children that came together in this garden. The money earned from their intricate toys made with the fibers of dwarf palm pays their schooling. The eighteenth-century screen, rescued from the demolition of a palace in Chaouen, was destined for a bread oven. As luck would have it, I happened to pass by. The chest is also from Chaouen, the most important center of painting on wood in northern Morocco.

PAGES 50–51: In the bedroom below the roof, the nineteenth-century iron bed is from England, made for exportation. In front, a painted chest made a few years ago in a village in the Rif region is proof that this old tradition has not disappeared. On the shelves of the bookcase are Moroccan straw breadbaskets and objects found on the beach and in local markets.

Nabil's Garden

Nabil's Garden consists of two terraces. The lower one, next to the house, is the home of two ancient olive trees. I found them in Tangier by the side of the road, uprooted by the excavators that were digging the foundations of a huge building. Using the chainsaw of a friend who had driven there quickly, I was forced to cut them down to the bone. The two bare stumps were hoisted up by a crane and later unloaded with a bang in the village nearest to us accessible to trucks. In those blessed years, to make the last two miles there was no other way but walking. By tying a number of poles between six mules — from packsaddle to packsaddle, from bridle bit to bridle bit, from back to back — we constructed a sort of animal machine not unlike the ones Native Americans of the prairies used to transport their dismantled tepees and possessions. It took us twelve hours to move the first tree. For the second tree we made it in less than ten — we were old hands now. That night we slept hard. Besides the two olive trees, with which I am madly in love (their crown is silver like God's long thick hair in Christian iconography), there are also a couple of echium plants, a philadelphus, and some roses.

The higher terrace is a broad expanse whose soil is a heavy whitish clay that around here is called *tafisa* — a nightmare for farmers. Years of spreading manure (mostly goat manure, which is more acid than that of cows and horses and has to be at least two or three years old) have somewhat improved its soil. Bracken mulch has also helped — we never remove it here. Lying at the heart and center of the Garden of Consolation, Nabil's Garden is directly above the Winter House, and I walk through it many times a day. Needless to say, I have a special affection for it. I'm sure gardeners will understand me — the most difficult spots of our garden are always those we love the most. Nature reminds us that no matter how much we try to tame her, in the end she is going to win. My advice is you take this philosophically and never forget it, if you want to become a gardener. As a matter of fact, to be a gardener is not a condition but an ongoing aspiration, a tension, halfway between prayer and sex — come to think of it, these two activities are quite similar.

Nabil is a young man full of good will who takes great care of his Garden. He is blond and muscular, with green eyes and regular features. I am pleased with this because a handsome youth looks good in the midst of the flowers. The first trees I planted here were a few citruses. These delicious lemon trees, "citron beldi" or Marrakech Limonetta, have grown well — unlike the orange and mandarin trees, but I don't plant them anymore, neither here nor anywhere else, because they are too demanding and prone to disease. In no other part of the garden have I made so many mistakes — out of anxiety, fear, and too many expectations. In the beginning I filled the flowerbeds with wild lavender planted formally in slanted rows. The small bushes all died within a few months. I learned to my cost that *Lavandula stoechas* prefers acid soil. I replaced it with species of rockrose that could tolerate limestone (*Cistus ladanifer*, *C. albidus*, *C. monspeliensis*, *C.* x *crispatus*, *C. creticus*, *C. libanotis*). However, rockroses don't live long, especially if they are planted amongst citrus trees that require abundant watering. After some years, among the few leggy survivors (to avoid lignification, rockroses should be pruned in the winter, but this is bad for their flowering) I planted a bit of everything, absolutely everything — with a preference for showy plants, as all together they produce the sort of orgiastic cacophony that I love in country gardens. I chose canna with variegated leaves and yellow, orange, pink, or vivid red flowers;

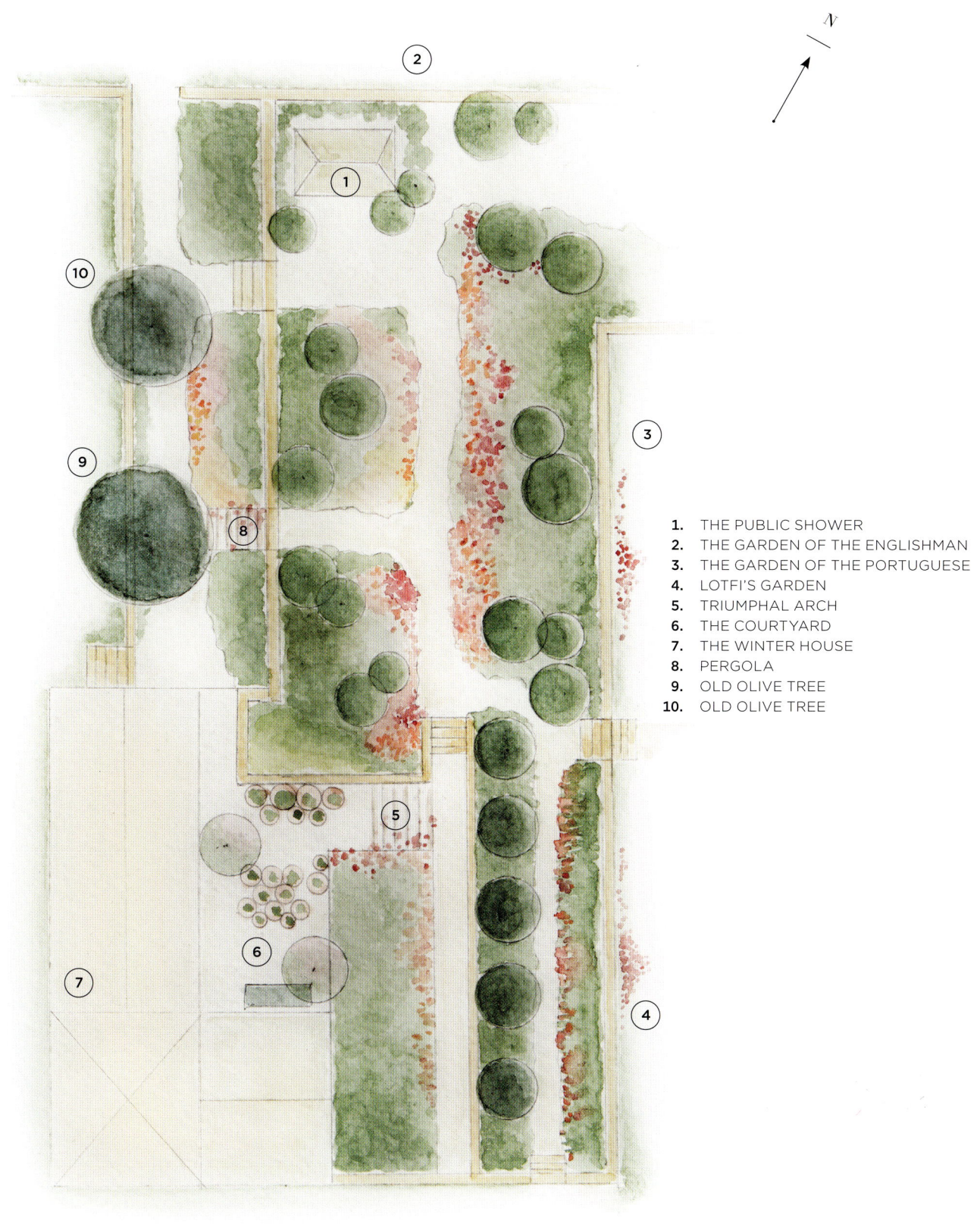

1. THE PUBLIC SHOWER
2. THE GARDEN OF THE ENGLISHMAN
3. THE GARDEN OF THE PORTUGUESE
4. LOTFI'S GARDEN
5. TRIUMPHAL ARCH
6. THE COURTYARD
7. THE WINTER HOUSE
8. PERGOLA
9. OLD OLIVE TREE
10. OLD OLIVE TREE

"black" sugar canes; and various *Melianthus major*, with fronds looking like ostrich plumes, whose seeds I had found on the outskirts of Tangier at the end of a lane — how those South African plants had ended up there is still a mystery to me. I added a dombeya, a *Romneya coulteri* (alas, the wonderful California tree poppy is still struggling), two *Aloe thraskii* looking like huge octopi with tentacles hemmed in pink, and two spectacular and prohibitive *A. barberae*. Then I delved into drought-tolerant sages, *Dahlia imperialis*, and *Echium fastuosum*, before discovering the infinite species of *Plectranthus* with leaves that range from pitch black to white through bronze and silver. I planted my beloved *Iresine herbstii*, which under this sun looks clad in rubies, and I gave the go-ahead to Bernard, who is not afraid of exoticism: in came a *Gardenia thunbergia* and a *G. volkensii*, with their fragrant summer flowers; a *Bauhinia tomentosa*, with its tiny inflorescences of a yellowish green much like the clusters of *Crotalaria agatiflora* (that belle of Mozambique who flowers in the same parterre); a snow-white *Ipomoea arborescens*; a bunch of red, yellow, and orange tecomas. And finally the oleanders took the stage — I had always been afraid of them but now I dared: simple and double, in pale yellow, fuchsia, Pompeian red, salmon, pale pink, and hot pink... I took and still take their cuttings here and there, even in hotel and gas station gardens, and in the flowerbeds of the superhighway. Oleanders are blessed; I still plant them among Sicilian euphorbias, South African pelargoniums, chubby crassulas, and fatal mysterious grasses I receive from gardener friends.

In short, I have found the key. I have also removed the paperwhites I had kept for winter blooming. I want Nabil's Garden to be garish in summer, and so I plant a great many annuals — dreamy *Verbena bonariensis* and down-to-earth zinnias, aristocratic cosmos and humble marigolds, melon- or saffron-hued tithonias, and black or albino sunflowers. In winter I like to see it rest beneath its blanket of mulch like a little boy asleep in his bed after running wild at a party. And maybe, who knows, through this turn-over of din and stillness, one day the soil will become that fine flour — loose and dark and with a light scent of mushrooms and chestnuts — we gardeners are all crazy about.

OPPOSITE: A border of *Dietes grandiflora*. When these South African plants in the Iridaceae family are in bloom, it seems as if a swarm of butterflies have alighted in the garden.

PAGES 56-57: Painted water jars, *Agave attenuata*, *Rosa* 'Madame Isaac Pereire' climbing on the wooden pergola, nasturtium: an old Moroccan garden.

PAGE 58: The public shower, where all our neighbors who don't have running water are welcome. **PAGE 59:** A bloom of *Gardenia thunbergia*. This is the perfume of paradise.

OPPOSITE: Two almond trees. In summer we eat their nuts with our cocktails.

PAGE 62: The only time I saw yellow oleanders in Morocco was in a gas station on the edge of Tangier. The attendant kindly let me take some cuttings, which fortunately rooted. Two months later, all the yellow oleanders at the gas station were replaced by double pink ones. **PAGE 63:** *Melianthus major* is generally cultivated for the beauty of its foliage. And what about its brown flowers that seem to be waiting to be nibbled by dinosaurs?

OPPOSITE: The Mexican flame vine (*Pseudogynoxys chenopodioides*) that drapes down the wall blooms for eight months of the year in this climate.

PAGE 66: The variegated foliage of *Canna indica* among the flowers of tithonia and zinnia. **PAGE 67:** The structure of wood posts and canes is typical of northern Morocco. Here it emphasizes the passage between two areas of the garden with different atmospheres.

BELOW: Left to right: *Dietes grandiflora*; *Tecoma stans* in a yellow hue that puts one in a good mood; *Salvia canariensis*; and a *Rosa* 'Sanguinea,' red like blood and like Snow White's apple.

The Garden of the Portuguese

In due time, this exotic terrace, planted by Bernard, will also become luxuriant. The day will come when to go down to the house we will have to open up a passage between the twisted branches of the schotia tree and the lacquer-hued crimson clusters of the *Erythrina herbacea*. To walk down the pathway that runs between the flowerbeds, we will have to duck beneath the foliage of the *Cassia candolleana* and brush up against the trunk of the *Cordia lutea* and the *Erythrina* x *bidwillii*. I cannot wait. João, the Portuguese dilettante (part botanist, part entomologist, and part archaeologist), for whom this part of my garden is named, is old and tired after all his travels. I built a bench for him. I was assisted by Najim, my carpenter friend, and by Soufien, our cook in Tangier. Ever since we left the city, rather than in elaborate meals Soufien has expressed his talent through the creation of wire trees and animals, vases covered in shells, and many other artefacts.

The seat of the bench is a patchwork of white marble fragments, while on all sides and on the back it is covered in ancient tiles and bits of tiles from Seville, Tunis, and Fez. It wouldn't look out of place in an aristocratic garden in Sintra or Lisbon.

Sometimes at nightfall I happen to see the Portuguese sitting there. His legs, clad in threadbare silken breeches, are crossed; from his open tailcoat I notice his torn yellowed jabot; his tricorne hat sags on one side. He smokes a pipe and looks out at the sea. I would love to be inside his head — if already he weren't in mine... His pale hand caresses the tiles. Half-closing his eyes, he sighs. Just like me, he has many interests and two whims: flower bulbs and old tiles. He also has a love, which is usually full of dash, but now, in the falling darkness, it has turned melancholic as all late loves are: this garden.

PAGE 71: A bench covered in sixteenth-century Sevillian tiles and fragments of Fez tiles from the same period.

PAGES 72–73: The young schotia and cassia trees, the euphorbias, and the aloes disappear under the red horde of the poppies.

OPPOSITE: The red lacquer of the *Erythrina* x *bidwillii* bloom evokes China.

BELOW: *Erythrina vespertilio* from Australia; *Ceiba insignis* from South America; *Cassia candolleana*, a native of Chile; and a *Tecoma* hybrid from the Americas. What in the world are these four exotic characters doing in this Moroccan country garden?

The Bone Garden

One day Bernard told me about his childhood dream of having a tree dressed in bones. It had always been a dream of mine too. In the garden I had a terrace where nothing much happened; a wild olive tree and a pomegranate grew there. We decided to transform it into an open-air curiosity cabinet. I spoke with the children of the village. I exchanged a few bank notes and got a pile of coins that sparkled in a dish like doubloons in a treasure trove.

To avoid the slightest hint of elegance in the manner of Georgia O'Keeffe's home — a risk even for a garden as cheerful as ours — the secret lay in quantity. Dogs, cats, rats, rabbits, goats, sheep, mules, donkeys, cows, bulls — many animals die in the fields. The children came loaded with bones, and walked away grasping in their hands those shiny pieces of metal that in a few minutes would turn into candy in the small local store. This is what I love about gardening — encouraging transformations.

It was fun. With the help of Nabil and Hamidou and the other gardeners, we began covering the trunk of the wild olive tree with skulls. On the branches we hung tinkling ladders of ribs and weighty pendants of tibias. We displayed garlands made of jawbones and fringes of vertebrae. On the ground, a lovely carpet of humeri and femurs. Then we went on with the setting. As in all the rooms I like, this one had to be open to every possibility. Using a big chunk of wood shaped like an ox skull and an old hardwood floorboard, we erected a totem pole to dance around it. For afternoon naps, there was one of Najim's beds made of arbutus wood. The dining table came from who knows where. We placed Bernard's collection of succulents on another table among the cussonias, cordylines, and *Tagetes lemmonii* we had just planted. And to prevent *them* from taking offense and wreaking havoc, we also arranged a nice cozy corner with two chairs bought in a café, in oleander wood painted in a dreamy green — ideal for country sprites in the mood for a tea among mortals.

The moon was full. The myoporum had been perfectly pruned by Bernard, and the view was open wide to the sea, as it had been once upon a time. Our neighbors were invited: old and young men, women, and children. The new room was a success. We had supper beneath the bones, like we still do in the hot summer evenings. Looking at the dim white glow radiating from the tree I thought: these animals are our ancestors; the tribe is reunited at last.

PAGE 78: If I were an olive tree, I would dress like this to go to a debutante ball.

PAGES 80-81: The outdoor living room. Actually, it is also a dining room, a ballroom, and a bedroom.

OPPOSITE: The tree of horns — created by Soufien, our cook in Tangier — with a post, some deer horns from the Rif, an empty gourd, and a few tillandsias.

PAGE 84: A totem is made with a plank of the floor in Tangier, which had come off after the rupture of a pipe that flooded the living room. The bucranium came from nearby woods, and the vertebrae from a field near the garden. **PAGE 85:** A bed for watching the stars.

The Garden of the Englishman

It was the first corner of the garden to have been given a name. Everything began by chance. In a landfill in Tangier, right where a colony of *Narcissus elegans* had flowered the autumn before, I found some *Crinum moorei* bulbs, with their ribbon leaves dry from the heat. I knew they love to drink but I took them to Rohuna anyway — we had water now. The fruit trees I had planted in the old orchard a few years earlier — pomegranate and almond trees, two peach trees, a plum tree — were now thriving and cast too much shade for tomatoes and aubergines to be kept there. So I decided to move the vegetable garden to a sunnier place, below what we now call Chinioui's Terraces. I gained a fine new room in a relatively fresh spot, roughly a hundred feet by sixty-five, surrounded by drystone walls and protected from the cold southwest winds by the high wall of our public shower. After years of the manuring needed for growing vegetables, the soil had become crumbly, dark.

With the tip of a reed, I traced out in the soil an area for armchairs and seats; then I drew out the path that would run around the central pergola. At the heart of our expanding garden — which at the time consisted almost only of indigenous species — this was a cozy space fit for reading and meditation, a small open-air study that looked like it had been there forever. I had proof of this one morning when I found Aisha sitting there. The frail mother of our old guardian, she came every once in a while to pick some aromatic herbs, like wild thyme, rosemary, and marjoram, that make her mint tea famous in the village. Dressed elegantly as usual, she sat on the ground with her shoulders against the wall. "*Assalamu alaikum*, Aisha. What's up?" She looked at me. "I was in the mood to think, so I have come here." "To think?" "Yes," she said, adjusting her headscarf with her shaky fingers full of rings. "Old places are good for thinking. The older the place, the better the thoughts."

The *Crinum moorei* were followed by *Crinum* x *powellii*, in abundance. In a small nursery I discovered a *Eupatorium sordidum*, a shrub with light purple powder-puff-like flowers that give a wistful feel to so many Mediterranean gardens. It would have been better suited to the climate of the Côte d'Azur, but I dared. Then some *Iris orientalis* in pale yellow and cream colors arrived from the garden of an acquaintance in Tangier who had sold his property to speculators. And now that everything — chirping birds, fluttering butterflies, shafts of light breaking through the blooming branches of fruit trees — created a soothing atmosphere of shade and peacefulness, of a timeless childhood garden, how could I resist planting those multi-colored daylilies, those little perfumed carnations, those yesterday-today-tomorrows (*Brunfelsia pauciflora* var *floribunda*) whose flowers are born violet and die white? How could I do without some cestrum, without the icy, Fanta-tinted spurt of streptosolen, without the joyous Sunday pealing of fuchsias? Or hedychium with its scent of ginger and of an old, gentle aunt? And why not a brugmansia? Or the alluring foliage of a *Vitex trifolia* 'Purpurea'? Or the blue flowers of sage? Or the rosy flowers of *Nicotiana mutabilis*, whose seeds, gifts from a friend, had germinated even if I didn't dare to transplant them because of the heat? How could I resist the perfume of a *Gardenia jasminoides*? Of hyacinths? Of horned violets?

It was clearly *them*, the *jennun*, who urged me, speaking within me with the voice of the old Englishman: "Don't worry. Go on dear boy." How bizarre: I was recreating the garden that had belonged (when? Who knows) to an elderly

Briton, and little by little I became acquainted with its former owner. Actually, he was quite stereotypical: an alcoholic, a lover of flowers who had cultivated them his whole life in the garden of his cottage — his strong suit was fritillaries, but alas! I simply have to forget them here. He was like so many expats I had come to know after moving to Tangier two decades before, except for two things: while most of his fellow countrymen were quiet people, he had retired to this remote country place in the wake of some sort of scandal. (I was not sure about that. It had something to do with a case of indecency. Sometimes the scene was a public urinal in a park with oaks and magnolias, at other times a boarding school dormitory with the night perfume of lime trees lazily entering through the open window.) Moreover, he lived within my brain.

Being next to our public shower attended by the men of the village, who sit in the garden and look at the flowers while awaiting their turn, the Garden of the Englishman (or the *Inglisi*, as we call it) has become popular and has sanctioned the state of madness of its creator. Hence, the family sayings — and habits — that make my relations with the gardeners so different from any other. As could be expected, many species had to be saved, just in time, by moving them to Tangier, which is milder and more humid, making way for dry-loving plants that could grow in Arizona or Andalusia — the romantic crinums have made it; they bloom in April, three months earlier than they should, and go dormant in summer, shedding all their leaves. But the gardener is always my old friend, my alter ego the *Inglisi*; after years of torrid summers, he has finally become familiar with plants he did not yet know when the Garden of Consolation began. Which more or less is what happened to me.

PAGE 86: At the feet of an old orange tree, a corner for reading.

OPPOSITE: Wild poppies (*Papaver rhoeas*) and opium poppies (*Papaver somniferum*) grow among tufts of *Iris orientalis*.

PAGES 90–91: A sitting room under an old fig tree, perfumed by gardenias in a bronze bucket that was formerly used in a *hammam*.

PAGE 92: In the foreground, pelargonium falls from the stone wall, mixing with *Justicia spicigera*. In the background, on the higher level, the leading character: *Rosa* 'Mutabilis'. **PAGE 93:** A corner of the pergola made of wood and wattle in the center of the Garden of the Englishman. This spot was built for the plants that love shade: ferns, clivia, and aspidistra.

BELOW: Left to right: *Bulbine frutescens* 'Hallmark'; *Tecoma garrocha*; *Iris orientalis*, formerly known as *Iris ochroleuca* — I love this iris so much that even though I have only known it in gardens, every time I see it in flower I imagine being in a swamp in Dalmatia, near a Macedonian stream, swimming with Alexander the Great; *Crinum* x *powellii* 'Album' in bloom.

The Exedra under the Fig Tree

The two important encounters in my adult life have been Stephan and this fig tree. I had been living with Stephan for fifteen years when I fell asleep under this tree. Since then we have grown older, all three of us. But the little country spirits that entered me during that slumber never grow older. Sometimes naughty little boys, sometimes decrepit giants bent with fatigue, the *jennun* live outside of time. (No, "live" isn't the right word. Even "exist" is too narrow for creatures that are as light as light and more solid than rock. I would venture to say "they laugh out green," which is what they do most frequently.)

When I woke and decided to move here, I thought that the first thing to do after building the hut was to transform the shady slope below the fig tree into a level exedra. I have never told anybody the reason why. The truth is that out of the corner of my eye I had seen a priest carrying a basket of apples under his arm. I believe this was in Provence. He was off to see someone. He was rather elderly, tired, sweating, and chubby, with a nice face. He sat down on the semicircular stone bench that enclosed this exedra and set down his basket. It was my duty of hospitality to give him a place to rest. I did so even before thinking to make a room for us. To offer him a glass of wine, like people in the countryside do for strangers, I absolutely had to build an exedra. Afterwards, everything would be alright.

It took an enormous effort to level the ground of the slope without damaging the centuries-old fig tree. Some of the boys used pickaxes, others shoveled and threw the dirt down the slope while another crew below us was building a drystone wall. To pack the earth down we danced upon it with our bare feet. I have never danced so much as in those nights, together with my new friends, to the song of the crickets. We shared the bread, the curdled milk they had brought from home, the tea that was now lukewarm in marmalade jars. Then we lay down to sleep under the stars, where it was less hot than in the hut.

After the exedra was finished that prankster priest didn't show up anymore. I now have only a dim memory of his visit, after years of breakfasts and lunches eaten in the balmy shade and suppers had in the Nativity-like light of the lantern I'd hung on a branch of the fig tree — before we had electricity, oil lamps made all the guests look like Georges de la Tour's Magdalene; years of meetings with gardeners, discussions, games, French and Darija lessons, of dealing household matters with Jelel, of drawing doodles for Najim; years spent around the different tables that have occupied the center of our exedra before falling apart. I went so far as to consider it a hallucination — obviously put on by *them*, who for whatever reason wanted to have a stone exedra for their meetings.

And meet they do, every night after we have gone to bed. Knowing their temper, I have planted only "easy" plants here, plants that are already part of the landscape and thus cannot disturb or irritate them. There is a border of *Dietes grandiflora*, the small South African iris that grows in every Tangier garden; a flowerbed of sage — to bread, fry, and serve as an appetizer — where in winter also some acanthuses grow — they have invaded all vacant lots of the region; a *Melia azedarach* like the ones you find on all pavements of the nearby towns; and a couple of Chinese roses, those *Rosa* 'Mutabilis' that are so happy here, obviously because *they* like them.

Since we began having supper in the Bone Garden, the *jennun* meet in the exedra a little earlier, while we are still eating. Only the *Inglisi* separates us from them. Sometimes I hear them whispering, and I crane my neck to see what in the world they are up to. I hear them laughing, shuffling, a sneeze, a yawn, the sudden cracking of a nutshell under a stone still warm from the sun… Even though Jelel always turns all the lights on, the table under the fig tree is invariably empty. Thankfully, over the years I have gotten used to it.

PAGE 96: The dining room under the fig tree.

PAGES 98–99: The exedra under the old fig tree. Here is where I slept the first time I came to Rohuna. Everything began here.

OPPOSITE: I have been trying for years to make a *Rosa* 'Mutabilis' climb on a *Melia azedarach*, the chinaberry tree. I think I am getting some result.

PAGE 102: The color of *Rosa* 'Mutabilis' changes from yellow to orange, then pink, and finally deep pinkish-red as the flower matures.

PAGE 103: On the pillars that mark the entry to the garden of the Exedra, stone vases from Salé contain two spherical stones found by the sea.

The Rotunda

Entering the garden through the gate marked by two plane trees, you can go left and then down to the Winter House, or straight ahead along the broad path, gently inclined toward the sea and shaded by three pines, which ends up in this rotunda. Once it was just a sandy slope. I wanted it to be a break between the blinding sunny outside and our liquid shades — it had to become a welcoming entrance where a person would be invited to linger for a while, resting and getting ready for adventure. The words of Vita Sackville-West rang in my mind: the structure of a garden must be formal, but the planting must be as informal as possible. Since the space was on a slope, the best shape for it — to create a harmony with the perspective — was an ellipse, which would give the illusion of a circle. I would enter its embrace and walk out of it feeling more confident, toward the terraces facing the sea.

To hide the irregularities that were inevitable in a path laid out by sight, I decided that the center of the circle should be filled with *Arundo donax*. These generous, hardy reeds, which the wind bends but does not break, must create a mass thick enough to prevent the sight of the imperfections in the dirt path that runs around them. Along the outer edge I put shorter plants such as perfumed pelargoniums (upon which climbs flaming clematis), viburnums, sansevierias, clivias, and variegated and American agaves, with myoporum, pittosporum, and yuccas in the background. In short, I used the same strategy as knock-kneed showgirls wearing fruit and embalmed birds on their heads. It is a trick that works in a garden.

I had been contacted by a group of Italian aid workers for the rehabilitation of a run-down neighborhood in the old *medina* of Tangier. I had to create a small garden in the main square. I hired some young men who spent their days waiting for tourists to fleece, and I brought them to a wasteland on the outskirts of the city. Amid rubble and garbage, I had them gather plants that would not need watering once they were established: rhizomes of *Arundo donax*, *Ipomoea indica* shoots, nasturtiums, castor-oil plants, and yellow daisies. To my surprise, after a couple of days, I learned that the residents of the neighborhood had uprooted everything, screaming that the *nazrani* was not a gardener but a thug, in cahoots with those other thugs who would have hidden behind the plants — whores, drunkards, dopeheads, *peligrosos* armed with knives! In their little garden they wanted to have pretty, "clean" plants, not the scrub that I had tried to foist on them!

Actually, "dirty" plants are my favorites. Especially since when Moroccan authorities made them disappear, replacing them with others — horribly neat and respectable — more suited to serve as a background to the phony rituals of power. Why have reeds always pleased me so much? Why do I like the castor-oil plants, with their large ruby-tinged leaves, that grow in the dust? Or acanthuses, peeking out of the stones of crumbling walls and transforming a pile of debris into the peristyle of a Corinthian temple? To tell you the truth, I find them sexy. They are all plants that unsettle and excite me (maybe the inhabitants of that neighborhood were not completely wrong). I love plants that remind me of dusty villages and love in the open-air, near the ditches, the trousers down, the feel of hot slippery mud against the skin. I love them, and I love to plant them in the garden.

The *Arundo donax* was consistent with the choice to use only indigenous plants. For years that big swaggering tuft placed at the entrance to our garden proclaimed my love for

a vanished Morocco (the carts, the little streams, the suburbs appearing like some sweet mirage) and made me shiver with excitement. But then we expanded, and thanks to abundant water I was able to dedicate myself to the Garden of Consolation, which became better organized, with more and more species being added. One day I realized that those reeds had become a little ostentatious, a sort of pose, like putting on a torn sweater to go to a dinner at the embassy. The garden was changing, and I had to cope with it.

I removed the reeds. In their place I planted some *Phormium tenax* — even if less ill-behaved, they reminded me of the wild girls who had been there before them. I added a couple of poinsettias (and took the opportunity to plant many more of them in the rest of the garden). I had never loved those Christmas stars; but in this climate, so similar to Mexico where they come from, their red and innocent bloom calls up a humble rural world — a little like the reeds do. I planted a group of *Agave attenuata* because their jade green makes all the other greens sing. Then came the *Aloe arborescens* that cover themselves in phallic orange cones; and a collection of sansevierias, with leaves like swords or tubes, or short and triangular like a mason's trowel — leaves of gray, lead-colored, delicate green, striped, or edged in white or yellow. But the whole still lacked height. I fixed the problem by planting two California peppertrees (*Schinus molle*) like the ones growing near every street intersection (luckily one of them was female — it was soon covered in berries). I also planted a jacaranda like the ones you see on local sidewalks. I was satisfied. No frills, much understatement, and the volume was right. And although the plants are not indigenous, they've been around for so long that they have become part of the landscape. I can't wait to find out what new changes the garden will force upon me.

PAGE 105: After some fifteen years, the *Pinus pinea* are beginning to assume their adult form.

PAGES 106–107: The Trojan Horse of our garden. We found it near our house.

OPPOSITE: Variegated agaves are often considered vulgar by gardeners and landscape designers. Evidently they have never looked at one of them with attention.

PAGES 110–111: All the hippeastrums planted in the ground come from local nurseries and are called in Morocco "beldi," meaning wild. They are evidently the descendants of the hybrids introduced in the 1920s by the French colonizers.

The Summer House

Describing happiness is impossible, but I'm trying anyway. During the first months it was a reed hut with a roof of palm leaves pressed together with clay. The roof was covered with a plastic sheet. Even though the choice we faced every evening was the same one that had tormented humankind since the Stone Age — die of cold or suffocate from smoke — we were always in good spirits. With eyes as red as rabbits, my new friends huddled around the fire and sang nostalgic songs. Then we talked and laughed until dawn.

A few months later, the hut had turned into a small stone house. Stephan and Sarah had arrived. The inside was dark, and it was difficult to make out scorpions and fat black (and probably deadly) tarantulas on the stones, so I had it whitewashed. I had never seen a more beautiful room: airy, full of rickety old beds, and oil lamps on the walls drawing cones of milky light and opalescent shadows. The ancient mosque of the village inspired some improvements: I added a porch supported by tapered pillars for eating outside, and palm leaves were replaced by a pitched roof covered with old tiles from Alicante. We were fed up with washing in the sea and using the bushes as a loo, so I gathered my courage and built a bathroom — outside, so as not to alter the perfect proportions of the room — with the shower fed by a plastic tank. The fresh water tasted of frogs, and the air smelt of sweet alison.

The first trees I planted were mimosas, *Acacia mearnsii*. They would grow quickly and quickly die as well, but their roots would hold the nitrogen in our sandy soil, paving the way for more long-lived plants. Nevertheless, growing takes time, and I am an impatient man. I had an idea: I drove a number of stakes into the ground. In each of them I stuck shorter stakes to which I hung all the stones with holes that I could find, tying them with the wonderful dwarf palm-fiber rope that is a local specialty. Stephan was a little puzzled by my stone trees, but I liked them. When you start making a garden, the small plants make you anxious and the waiting is frustrating, so it is vital to award yourselves some consolation prizes. My prizes were all the things I brought home with the help of my gardeners: the twisted trunks of dead olive trees; a bronze cannonball found on a nearby beach at the foot of that cliff with a small Spanish fortress on top; stones that look like fragments of statues of Romans in togas; balls of limestone from a cave; roots; wooden planks from a shipwreck; old tires to be white-washed with limestone. In the meantime, I transplanted *Iris tingitana* bulbs and watered the first pelargoniums with our only saucepan.

I was living here by now. The garden wanted me to. I began to build the Winter House. The house where we had been living automatically became the Summer House. Back then, who could have imagined that our old hut would one day have its own kitchen, direct access to the loo, running water, a large stove, and all the conveniences? Yet making a garden means getting closer and closer to nature, gently imposing our presence on her. But I have to confess: now that our garden is green and luxuriant, I am not as happy as I was in those days long ago, except when I wander in a scorched field with just small thyme bushes, and my eyes, finding no point of rest, are drawn into the abyss of the valley, of the sea. Not that I regret anything. I have learned to resist the temptation to erect my stone trees. The garden has taught me that.

PAGE 113: The terrace of the Summer House, whose pillars were copied from the old village mosque, which has since been destroyed.

PAGES 114-115: In the Summer House is the only room here that has four beds: two double and two single. When the kids from Darna (an organization staging theatre performances with street children in Tangier) come to Rohuna, the little ones sleep here. If they lie crosswise, we can have sixteen kids sleeping on the four beds.

BELOW: Details of the Summer House's terrace. The stripe fabrics are *mendil*; the women wear them wrapped around their waists or knotted over their shoulders to carry wood, children, and water containers.

The Wild Room

It is a small room in the middle of the garden, about thirty by twenty-five feet. It lies between the Garden of the Englishman and the Garden of the Italian. Its only tree is an old fig tree that was already there. This is where I planted my first wild flower bulbs: narcissi and irises, which have done well in the poor soil. After they have finished blooming, out come all the plants that reseeded themselves from the year before, as well as the ones carried in by the birds and the wind. The strongest survive, and they are not necessarily the most beautiful: sterile oats, thistles, vetch, and chicory — scrub. When we are lucky, we have some mullein and carrots. Now that we have so much space to plant the indigenous bulbs, it would probably be more sensible to use this room for other purposes. For several months of the year, these tall graceless stalks block views that would be the pride of any gardener: the agapanthuses in bloom in the Garden of the Italian, which from the Garden of the Englishman look like a sunny lake; the tecomarias and tecomas in the Garden of the Englishman, which from the Garden of the Italian are a multi-colored waterfall. Many visitors, after politely asking what is the purpose of this space, suggest I eliminate it. I never will. I am fond of our Wild Room. I love it in October with the blooming of the first *Narcissus viridiflorus*, which I found in Tangier between the graves in the cemetery of Boubana — if I planted them among other bulbs, how would I recognize these old narcissi that, with their little songs, inspired one of the few stories of which I am proud? I love it in January when the *Iris tingitana* (perhaps because they are lonely, isolated) shout to my face their courage of young warriors who have come down from the mountains to conquer the world; they remind me of how happy I felt the first time I discovered them — an endless array of youths with helmets crowned with crests as blue as the sea. And I love it in the spring when so many common plants, apparently clumsy, taint the picturesque harmony of the Garden of Consolation. I draw near, I bend over and observe them. Hairs, thorns, epithelium, scales, cilia. I think of the frog who becomes a prince. No need for a kiss. Just observe them carefully, and the miracle happens once again.

OPPOSITE: *Galactites tomentosa* and *Glebionis coronaria* running rampant in the Wild Room.

PAGES 120–121: A fig tree and weeds: my kind of garden.

Stephan's Terrace

This was my surprise to Stephan. After drilling the first well found by his dowser cousin, a twelve-year-old girl, we dug a tank to collect water from it. Later I had it covered with cement, and in the cement I anchored posts for making a pergola. I planted honeysuckle, whose strong roots spread everywhere. On the wild olive tree of the nearby Bone Garden climbed a buddleia and a *Rosa gigantea* hybrid, a rose called 'La Follette'. Like all roses descending from their vigorous Himalayan ancestor, it has beautiful bronze foliage, loves the heat, and grows rapidly. I pulled a few branches onto the pergola. In a couple years, the shade would become as dense as in a forest.

Stephan was very pleased with his surprise when he arrived for his summer holiday. At sunset, on the terrace overlooking the valley and the ocean, we played "who's-the-painter": there were the golden mists by Turner; the clouds by Courbet; the rosy white marbling effects by Mantegna; and those more vivid by the Venetian Renaissance masters Titian and Giovanni Bellini. To the east, where the light was dying, it was the sky of a melancholy pastoral scene by Watteau. But looking at the sun, it was melted gold, the background of molten metal, liquid and glowing, of a Salome by Gustave Moreau. In the afternoon, having made our way back on foot from the beach, we invited a dozen children for a snack, in the shade of a sheet stretched between the posts that were still bare. I had bought a gas refrigerator. None of our guests had ever tasted a cold beverage. Ah, those icy cold Coca-Colas gulped while sweaty and panting...

As darkness fell, Jelel brought supper. I had got to know him on the beach. He was the only one of our young men who went to Tangier to work every Sunday afternoon with his backpack on his shoulder. He had been a fisherman since he was thirteen. I thought that a young man who was used to living alone on a boat, far from his family, would be a good caretaker for our house — I was not wrong. Jelel is now married to Nabia, has three children and some gray at his temples. He still lives and works with us.

Here we had supper all together, guests and gardeners, seated on a mat, sometimes accompanied by the violin of Abdelillah, our local Paganini who performed at weddings. Then the stars. Then we went to bed. Stephan had some beds carried out onto his terrace. On hot nights we slept there.

Today we spend less time on Stephan's Terrace. A rich Frenchman's polo grounds, incongruously green, are a plague in the view. This has become a passageway between the Bone Garden and Chinioui's Terraces. I only put a few pots for the summer: marigolds, cosmos, and the *Hibiscus moscheutos* and *Salvia uliginosa* I cannot do without; they do need a great deal of water, but if the pot is in a big bowl always full of water, they bloom just like in the marshes from where they come. This concentration of semi-aquatic plants must have something to do with the first well dug here and with all my illusions that were bitterly shattered by its stinginess. At the foot of the terrace, toward the sea, I dug another tank. I filled it with soil and planted it with calla lilies and yellow flag irises (*Iris pseudacorus*) that had had the misfortune of growing in the wrong pond, in the path of the new motorway. Then I poured in a lot of water. Near the tank, in the dry soil, I planted about a hundred *Iris filifolia*. Placing drought-tolerant plants next to those that need plenty of water might seem the perversion of a gardener in need of special effects. But when the white callas, the golden *Iris pseudacorus*, and the purple *Iris filifolia* all blossom together, they make me want to play "who's-the-painter" also when I am in the garden. Now, for instance, I am right in the middle of a fresco by Pontormo.

PAGE 123: Najim's neo-Gothic chair is caressed by the vigorous rose 'La Follette', which would be able to envelop it in two seasons, and crush it in four.

PAGES 124–125: On Stephan's Terrace we have gazed at thousands of sunsets, and drunk as many gin and tonics.

OPPOSITE: An oleander, proud of its Pompeian red.

Chinioui's Terraces

Chinioui is Lotfi's older brother. He was a couple of years old when I moved here. When he was six he had a nasty case of pneumonia. To prevent him from catching cold, and his father from going every day all the way to the hospital — miles and miles on the back of his mule with him on his lap — I offered to give him his shots. I rubbed him energetically with a cotton wad soaked with alcohol; and when he turned his worried face toward me to ask "How much longer," I had already finished injecting the antibiotic. Being both fond of animals, Chinioui and I were meant to become friends: he slept with a tiny owl between his neck and shoulder and was inseparable from his little lamb; I dined every evening with a drunken praying mantis. But when he turned eight, my friend Sarah and I decided that he and his little brother should begin attending a real school, not the one held in the mosque annex where the *fqih* taught only the Qu'ran. We brought them to Tangier, rented a room at the home of their greedy uncle who is a tailor, and enrolled them in the neighborhood school. Every Friday afternoon, when we brought them home, it was a celebration. But on Sunday evenings, while Lotfi stood ready with his satchel in his hand, there was no sign of Chinioui. He'd cut and run. He wandered through ravines and valleys holding his little lamb in his arms. Some relative or other always managed to capture him. And it was indeed a tiny wild animal torn from its land, the sobbing kid that Sarah and I, with lumps in our throats, forced ourselves to bring back to the city. When he was sixteen, he left school and became an apprentice to an auto electrician. But it was an odd job and paid a pittance. When his father stopped working here, I asked Chinioui to take over for him. Having spent his childhood playing between our flowerbeds, he was certainly familiar with plants. And I could use a gardener who was able to read our alphabet — he reads with some difficulty, but you can't expect too much from Moroccan public education.

Chinioui's flowerbeds were planted with fruit trees: mulberries, apricots, figs, pomegranates, a couple of quinces and pears. They were all bordered with rosemary — at the time of my foolhardy beginnings, this blessed unassuming plant had helped to protect me from the boundless space of the valley, which was more suited to the revelation of a god than to human life. With the years, and although we regularly pruned it, the rosemary had become leggy. If we tried to prune it harder, cutting into the wood, it died. I couldn't stand the sight of those knotty, bare legs anymore. I decided to uproot it. While I was at it, I also got rid of all the honeysuckle that covered the drystone walls. You could spend an entire week cutting it back, and in no time its vigorous shoots would have already wrapped themselves around the trees, threatening to suffocate them. It had become a Sisyphean task. After more than fifteen years, I felt as if I hadn't accomplished anything: all I had here were a few shrubs and a few fruit trees struggling to survive in a clay that was impervious to water and wretchedly poor, despite all the sand and manure we had thrown into it.

But the mulch suggested by Bernard, and the ardor with which Chinioui applied it (an ardor a tad excessive sometimes, on account of his immoderate consumption of *kif*) have done wonders. The soil opened up. Agapanthuses and canna lilies are so thrilled with the feast of earthworms around their roots that, content with the sunlight they have absorbed during the winter, they flower in the middle of summer, despite a dense shade that would be more suitable to ferns. Our old, mangy lantanas are now fireworks of flowers; their dim foliage highlights the long transparent leaves of the canna lilies that filter the light. At the foot of

1. STEPHAN'S OLIVE TREE
2. PERGOLA
3. THE GARDEN OF THE ITALIAN
4. THE WILD ROOM
5. STEPHAN'S TERRACE
6. THE LOWER TERRACE
7. THE UPPER TERRACE

the lantanas there is a medieval tapestry of pink tulbaghias; orange and yellow bulbines; red, purple, crimson, violet pelargonium hybrids; and many pink and white *Matthiola incana*. The *Euryops pectinatus* in this climate are covered by golden daisies eight months of the year — together with the Canary Island daisies they look like clouds of cherubs clustered around the Madonna who is rising up to heaven.

In the shade of the violet-colored vitex that sneaks in among the branches of the fig trees (each one with its pale rose, progeny of the *Rosa gigantea*), we have planted *Convolvulus sabatius*, little flowers of an ineffable violet color, and silver-leaved *Helichrysum petiolare*. They creep toward the drystone wall, climb it, and drip down in waterfalls, to receive the kiss of the sun. The effect is a bit too elegant, but it is moderated by the rustic, red-orange flowers of the Mexican flame vine (*Pseudogynoxys chenopodioides*).

In the few remaining patches of sun, Bernard couldn't resist planting a noble *Cordia boissieri* and a couple of South American daisy trees, with their dark foliage which is a joy in itself (*Montanoa tomentosa*, *M. bipinnatifida*, and *M. hibiscifolia*). I added some *Tithonia diversifolia* and several *Tagetes lemmonii* — I absolutely want some winter flowerings here. Chinioui often comes with us to the small nurseries in the region, where among scratching chickens and cooing turtledoves it's always possible to discover a treasure. He is the one who chooses the plants that tickle his fancy and decides where to plant them. With confident taste, he surrounds the orange strelitzias with violet osteospermum; he interweaves the canary-yellow osteospermum with copper- and wine-colored gazanias; he sinks the low branches of the *Hibiscus syriacus* under the big silver wig of the *Echium fastuosum*; he places red gauras among the Spanish brooms and white gauras at the feet of the *Lycianthes rantonnetii*. Although, as one might have guessed, there is not much room left for annuals in these flower beds — I just can't do without violet and cherry-syrup red cinerarias, my opium poppies (*Papaver somniferum*), and a few red fennels (*Foeniculum vulgare* 'Bronze') that go so well with the blue leaves of thistles and sage. And when in November or December the tiny hollyhocks are ready to be transplanted, it was Chinioui's idea to plant them all over — between the crassulas and the bidens, amid the tufts of clivia and crinum, and right next to the trees, where they vigorously grow in winter. Then, as the shade gets denser and denser, they begin to climb toward the skies. In the spring they become towers of garnet, amethyst, pearl white, and pink, reaching up to twenty-five feet — I have measured them! For a novice gardener, Chinioui is quite promising.

PAGES 130–131: In the lower terrace, facing the valley, hippeastrum, *Echium fastuosum*, and *Tagetes lemmonii* flower between the young black fig trees from Chaouen — in the Rif region alone there are more than one hundred and fifty varieties of figs, each assigned with its own name.

OPPOSITE: A corner of the same terrace. The rose that climbs on the pear tree is one of the damask cultivars grown by the peasants in the region. It flowers only once a year, and if the sun is too strong, they only last a couple of weeks. But it's worth it.

PAGE 134: *Melianthus major*, *Echium fastuosum*, *Bulbine frutescens*, and pelargonium blooming among olive and pomegranate trees.

PAGE 135: Many years ago a friend who worked at Great Dixter gave me a little bulb of this fragrant *Gladiolus tristis* that came from the greenhouse of the famous English garden. It's made itself at home here in Rohuna: it has vigorously multiplied and every year, despite its name, it flowers quite happily.

PAGE 136: At the bottom of the steps connecting the two terraces is the *Rosa* 'Rose de Rescht', an old rose which was once considered of Persian origin but is more likely French instead, brought to Iran in the early 1800s and rediscovered in the provincial capital of Rescht after World War II. A cutting of this rose was given to me by David Herbert, second son of the Earl of Pembroke and the doyen of the expat community in Tangier. Persia, France, England, Morocco: in this stretch of the garden, I like to welcome cosmopolitan creatures. The strelitzia plants are still too young to flower; one has to be patient with these birds of paradise. **PAGE 137:** Echiums, lavenders, olive trees: the symphony of grays from these Mediterranean plants is counterpointed by the tender green foliage of the pomegranate.

OPPOSITE: The sun peeps through the branches of a fig tree: the *jennun* are humming a simple tune.

PAGES 140–141: I don't know why but the border of *Dietes grandilora* makes me think of Chekhov. The boys call the wooden support for the climbing roses "amaria" — it is the name of the canopy, hoisted on a mule, used to transport a bride to her husband's house on their wedding night.

PAGE 142: *Pelargonium zonale* is mixed with *Dietes grandiflora* right at the bottom of a mulberry tree.
PAGE 143: *Rosa banksiae* 'Lutea', my favorite among the banksia roses, bloom on a wooden trellis. Thousands of canaries in love — and a Merovingian enamel in the solid blue of the sky.
PAGE 144: The quince tree in fruit. Every year we make large quantities of a delicious quince jam. Together with bread cooked in our oven and mint tea, it's the snack we all enjoy at 10 o'clock in the morning. **PAGE 145:** Lantana, tulbaghia, oleander, stock: plants that are as common as the rhyme between love and dove. The young trees are growing.
OPPOSITE: First row, left to right: *Cordia boissieri*; *Bidens heterophylla*; a double hibiscus that changes color from white to pink as it matures. Second row: Matthiola; tulbaghia; cineraria (*Pericallis* x *hybrida*), the same ones cultivated by our grandmothers, happy in this African garden. Third row: Copper gazania, unique among the colors in the garden and capable of giving an electric shock to its neighboring flowers; a *Rosa Gigantea* hybrid; *Leucophyllum frutescens*, the drought-tolerant Texas sage whose pink blooms are triggered by rains.

The Garden of the Italian

You couldn't imagine a simpler structure than this terrace where I once grew zinnias for cutting. Two crossing paths creating four beds where young olive trees are planted, interspersed with myrtle bushes, and with agapanthuses used as ground cover. At the intersection point, I put four oleanders and four groups of *Iris orientalis*. It is like the design of a six-year-old boy. And yet, it is one of the corners of the garden where I spend the most time. Seated in a chair made by Najim, I manage to read, take notes, and sometimes even draw something. There are few distractions here. When my eyes look up from the page, they see only plants they have always known — the holiday plants of an Italian childhood. The oleanders are pink and double, with the exception of one that is white; unfortunately, in Morocco, there is no way you can trust the nursery — and you have to plant them before they carry the blooms. This garden has the same mood and the same perfume of my childhood siestas, outdoor games, *merende* — it reminds me of those strolls with a sweater on my shoulder, of those ice creams after dinner...

The trees in Chinioui's Terraces cover the magnificent view. What a rest it is, every now and then, to forget the gods and to bask in our condition of pensive primates! So as to recall that even the human race has a history that is glorious in its own way, I built a bench and placed it against a wall supporting the upper garden, Hamidou's Garden. I encrusted the bench with fragments of pottery. There are splinters of turquoise glass paste from Saqqara, from the desert of Luxor, from Memphis; little pieces of Roman dishes from Appia Antica and the Palatine; Byzantine and Seljuq shards that I put in my pockets in Anatolia and Syria; Fatimid, Ayyubid and Mameluke souvenirs from those poignant afternoons spent wandering through Cairo's necropoles; a fragment of a sixteenth-century tile given to me by a Portuguese monk; the broken faience tiles that my mother gave me to support my precocious passion; a couple of medieval Fez tiles with inscriptions on them; two or three other Fez tiles from a later time — I managed to recover them from a pile of debris during the restoration of an old palace — decorated with those expertly naive floral patterns that make Moroccan ceramics so special. On the sides of the bench I put pieces of unglazed earthenware from three Phoenician tombs I discovered behind the dunes of our valley. I notified the authorities, but to no avail, and so the *nazrani*'s bulldozers, while digging his polo grounds, have wiped out the tombs and a couple of surface Neolithic sites as well — some of its hatchets and arrow heads are now in my living room. Thankfully, some years before I had got myself the old French and Spanish archeological maps on which the colonizers had meticulously and affectionately marked the ancient remains of this poor country.

Being a résumé of the history of Mediterranean ceramics, this bench has the power to console me when I am sad or worried about the future of our village in a country that has lost its memory. The plants console me just as much, because they are not your typical *garden plants*; they were not chosen and displayed for the sake of the effect (but when the agapanthuses are in bloom the effect is nonetheless spectacular); they seem to have been placed here and in this way by someone who knows little about such things, and who only wants to sit in the open air and enjoy the shade, reading and dreaming. As a matter of fact, the Garden of the Italian is the most consoling part of the Garden of Consolation.

PAGE 148: A water jar at the end of two flowerbeds with agapanthuses and myrtles.

PAGES 150–151: I planted these olive trees when they were twenty inches high. Today I read while sitting in their shade.

OPPOSITE: This small sitting area owes its perfume to the double oleanders. It is the typical scent of an Italian childhood's holidays.

PAGE 154: The history of ceramics around the Mediterranean on a small bench whose back is made of three seventeenth-century Moroccan tombstones.

PAGE 155: *Sic transit gloria mundi.* There is much beauty even in the end.

PAGE 156: From bottom to top: Ceramics from eighteenth-century Morocco, the Italian Renaissance, and pieces from Ptolemaic and Roman Egypt. They are all encrusted around a fragment of medieval epigraphic tile from Fez.

PAGE 157: On two whale vertebrae, painted in turquoise and found in a house in the village where they served as stools, is a big bronze pot that was once used to cook the soldiers' ration. Now it holds *Narcissus* 'Tête-à-tête' in the spring and marigolds in the summer.

BELOW: Acanthus, agapanthus, aeonium in pots, and double oleanders among myrtles and olive trees: the typical Italian garden by the sea in the 1960s.

Hamidou's Garden

The garden that lies before the Summer House was the first of Rohuna's gardens. Twenty years ago, while I was still living in a hut, I began planting in the sand the large rockroses *(Cistus ladanifer)* that grew along the road between Tangier and Cape Spartel. I had never seen such tall rockroses (they can reach twelve to fourteen feet). I learned afterwards that this is an endemic variety that attracted botanists from all over the world. Sadly, due to the widening of the road and the new buildings, their number has dramatically decreased. Among the rockroses, I planted the yellow daisies from Tangier's wastelands *(Glebionis segetum)*, and added the first Spanish broom, scillas, and spurges. The boys were building a retaining wall over three hundred feet long to keep the newly spread topsoil from being washed away by the impending autumn rains. Meanwhile, in the mad chirping of the cicadas, I was laboring on this large, sun-scorched terrace, the sweat running into my eyes and my head spinning. I realized that if I wanted to survive I had to have shade. I chose mimosas. They are not indigenous to Morocco, but they have been around for so many years that they feel perfectly at home here, just like the prickly pears, eucalyptuses, maritime pines, and myoporum. They would grow quickly, and their roots would enrich the soil with nitrogen.

Two years later, while our hut was turning into a little house, the mimosas (*Acacia mearnsii, A. longifolia, A. saligna, A. podalyriifolia*) were already small trees about six feet tall. During the third summer, we all slept together in our large room made of stone, and we could spend our days in the fragrant shade of the mimosas.

The onset of shade in a place that has never known it (or has lost it decades ago on account of man) has unpredictable consequences. In the evenings, my beloved toads came by the hundreds. Sometimes, on a leaf of maize, I would encounter an emerald-colored tree frog, and my heart beat with joy. Then hedgehogs arrived. The grass snakes fled to the flowerbeds in search of coolness; the butterflies mated and deposited their eggs. And seeds that would have gone up in smoke in the blazing sun were now germinating: tiny oleanders and viburnums as well as *Mirabilis jalapa*. The news spread in the village. Gifts began to arrive. There were dog rose cuttings that had been culled in the forest; rhizomes of canna lilies from the local courtyards; *Iris belouini* from the little cemetery behind the mosque; medlar and fig seedlings that had traveled from the *souk*, their root balls wrapped in rags, inside a straw bag gripped tightly in the donor's lap, or between rubber boots and sardines rolled up in paper. There were also young strawberry trees; fat, poisonous sea squill bulbs; broad beans; and Jerusalem artichoke, carrot, and cabbage seeds. In addition, autumn daisies and scillas were brought to me by children, who became less shy every day. Thanks to the mimosas, this scorched patch of land was becoming a place of connections and exchanges between human beings, plants, and animals, which is what any garden worthy of the name should be. I began to plant with enthusiasm: a row of pomegranate trees to protect our open-air living room from the east wind, chinaberry trees and mulberries, olive and pear trees, Phoenician junipers and pittosporums — and my stone trees as well — in order to create more and more shade. I planted, and I planted. I simply could not stop.

A couple of years later, Hamidou's Garden was already known among us as "The Shade Garden" and among the villagers as "*El Rhaba*" — the forest. It had indeed the charm

1. LUXOR
2. NAJIM'S BRIDGE
3. THE SUMMER HOUSE
4. THE GARDEN OF THE ITALIAN

of a northern Moroccan forest with its flowery clearings which welcome you after you've crossed the thorny brushwood — the same perfumes, the same chirping of birds. The *jennun* were so happy. I had an idea: promoting an encounter between different worlds. Why shouldn't I introduce a couple of beautiful nymphs to the genies of the place? Yes, nymphs — those lovers of damp paths, the epigeal creatures and dryads of our Italian woods. In order to lure them here (or to evoke them, as somebody might say — somebody who will never see them), I provided the first sansevierias with hundreds of their sisters, which looked straight out of a courtyard of a Neapolitan baroque palazzo. I planted butcher's brooms with scarlet berries; among the butcher's brooms I planted their cousin, *Danae racemosa*, the sweetheart of Zeus. I indulged in my love for clivias, encircling the first ones with more clivias, and on and on. When the flowers blossomed, those broad expanses turned orange like ponds full of evening light. Around the edge I planted some cordylines with delicate leaves cascading down as water from a fountain. In the empty spaces I put bracken and Boston ferns, *Iris foetidissima* with berries full of coral-colored seeds, asparagus with feathery fronds, dwarf fan palms, trunks of dead olive trees, species of aloes that flourish in the shade, ancient jars, chairs, carved stones.

But the nymphs, who in the beginning were eager and full of hope, soon interrupted their games. The *jennun*, accustomed to the lunar barrenness of these landscapes, had initially regarded them with bland curiosity. But they grew tired of the nymphs' noisy dances. They became sarcastic and then downright rude. The shade was too much for their taste. By their nature, the mimosas do not live long. In no time at all, the *jennun* sucked off their lymph. I had to have them cut down. And while a procession of nymphs fled hastily (to keep their bare white skin from being sunburnt they ran so fast that it was difficult to see them), the garden became sunny again. It got back to where it started: scorching heat, and cicadas.

I had to remove almost everything and relocate the plants into the shade that in the meantime had finally settled down in Chinioui's garden. Hamidou's large terrace has not yet found its proper face. Sure, the California pepper tree (*Schinus molle*) and jacarandas grow better thanks to the nitrogen in the soil; the aeonium*s* and cotyledons are a help; no doubt the two *Tipuana tipu*, the *Phytolacca dioica*, James McBey's *Euphorbia tirucalli* that Christopher gave me, those *Euphorbia candelabrum*, and hibiscuses, kalanchoes, viburnums, hippeastrums, kentia and many other species of palms — they are all happy in the blazing sun. But that is not enough. Should I plant cork trees? Holm oaks? More strawberry trees? I am at a loss. I miss the nymphs and their celebrations. And I so wish that my *jennun* were more hospitable. When I complain about their bad temper, Hamidou (the oldest and most experienced gardener) says to me: "You can't help it. They are country spirits, they have their ways. Shouldn't you be grateful to them for accepting you? You did know mimosas are short-lived." So I look around and marvel at the miracle of this garden where once there were only stones. And in my heart, I thank the *jennun*, I thank them every day — those solitary peasant spirits who teach me the humility and patience of a gardener.

OPPOSITE: A bench by Najim in painted arbutus wood.

PAGES 164–165: A red sitting room by Najim. The euphorbias that were searching for light in this shady garden grew crooked, and I liked them that way. I knew that the mimosas (*Acacia mearnsii*) planted to provide shade and fix nitrogen in the soil would soon be dead, allowing the euphorbias, as well as the palms, to grow lush.

PAGE 166: Mimosa blooms.

PAGE 167: Sansevieria, aeonium, and *Pelargonium zonale* with their red blooms.

OPPOSITE: Native to almost all the countries around the Mediterranean, *Iris foetidissima* prefers shade.

PAGE 170–171: This terrace in Hamidou's Garden is called Luxor, or The Garden of the Egyptian. The bench was one of the old furnishings in the garden of La Mamounia in Marrakech, before that marvelous hotel was renovated — and made commonplace. Here one can come to smoke *habli babli* in the company of a Cairo gentleman of Sudanese origin, made of smoke and shadow.

PAGES 172–173: Even though they are not indigenous, the mimosas are by now a part of the landscape of northern Morocco. This corner of the garden recreates a forest around Tangier from about thirty years ago.

BELOW: From left to right: The yellow clivia is for me like a fairy with blue hair; the *Cistus ladanifer* from Cap Spartel can reach up to fourteen feet in height; *Billbergia nutans* performs its miracle; how many of us have seen the bashful and cheeky flower of a sansevieria?

THE WILD GARDEN

The heart of the garden beats here, in this apparently uncultivated strip of land that surrounds the Garden of Consolation. These indigenous plants, which have been rescued from construction sites, have not been watered for years because they don't need to be. If they look like they have blossomed and grown here it's because they really might have — before the goats wiped the slate clean with their gluttony, and before man delivered the final blow by digging up and burning all roots to make coal to sell at the *souk*. Every time my elderly neighbors tell me about the valley of their childhood sixty or seventy years ago, I think: man is the most ruthless enemy to the world. Our stony slope — and the eyes of these old men, clouded by cataracts, take on a dreamy sweetness — was then a forest of majestic mastic trees as tall as the minaret of our mosque. Here grew the *buchannu*, the strawberry trees, and the *guermesh*, the viburnums used to make the *sebsi*, the small wooden pipes for smoking *kif*. Down there — and a finger bent by arthritis and yellowed by tobacco indicates the ocean — the dunes were contained by a thick barrier of trees and bushes that prevented the sand from invading the fertile land. There were less people then. Everyone grew his own vegetable garden and his own orchard, irrigated with the water of the river that today is siphoned off by the rich *nazrani* for his polo grounds. They could let their fields lie fallow then, and there were uncultivated expanses where the "onions" (as they call the bulbs in this region) blossomed.

My sadness is softened by my gratitude to the *jennun*, the genies who have guided me. Indeed, I would like to be able to work on a larger scale, to give back to this land what has been taken from it. To replant the entire valley, to see it become full of flowers and verdant again — trees and trees, and fresh shades for the animals, and feasts of birds... It would be like walking on air for me. But I am happy anyway. Disdainfully fleeing human settlements, the *jennun* have found peace and shelter in our little oasis, among the ruddy cork trees and the carobs, where the air smells like mint, thyme, oregano, and rosemary. In December I am in my ideal garden. The strawberry trees are covered in small fruits of a Snow-White red; the *Clematis cirrhosa* festoons the viburnums loaded with metallic berries; the clearings are full of paperwhite narcissi scented like orange blossom. And I hear the *jennun* laughing out like they do, laughing out green, with a rustling that sounds like the wind among the branches. Yet it is in spring, in our deafening North African spring, that I see them. Between March and May, the *jennun* become children — as tall as irises, and as slender, as slouching, their helmets crested in purple. When the sun rises, they begin their wild dances among the pink, white, and yellow rockroses, among the garlics and the scillas, among the mulleins bobbing their heads, and the orchids offering theirs to the bees, and the gladioli bowing theirs, and the ornithogalums.

PAGES 176–177: *Ornithogalum arabicum* in bloom among the mastic trees and euphorbias from the Canary Islands. To the right there is Bab el Bahr, the Sea Gate onto the path that leads to the beach.

PAGE 178: When the arbutus trees are covered in their scarlet fruits, and the paperwhite narcissi are blooming, the *jennun*, the spirits of the forest, go wild with joy.

OPPOSITE: Rockroses, mastic shrubs, and santolina around the cabana near the Sea Gate.

PAGES 182–183: Stephan's Olive Tree, masterfully pruned and tidied by Chinioui and Nabil. I am proud of them.

BELOW: If for some absurd reason I had to declare which is my favorite plant, I would say *Arbutus unedo*. The shiny foliage is the most beautiful green in nature. The waxy flowers and the red fruits are on the branches at the same time. Rockroses and many indigenous bulbs, including ornithogalum, bloom between the trunks of the arbutus.

THE GHARSA BAQQALI

It is my paradise. A hill that slopes gently down into a shallow basin with an ancient stand of fig trees; then a gully, then another hill. A reddish and flaxen landscape that looks like the scene of the creation of the world; down yonder, lies the sea. The Gharsa Baqqali borders our garden and is separated from it by a public footpath, over which there is a wooden bridge that Najim made for me. It used to be the only garden in Rohuna, the only place where wood for burning was cut sparingly and goats were not allowed to graze. In virtue of the so-called regime of joint property, it belonged to 157 persons. Only someone who is familiar with the complexity of Moroccan rural property laws can conceive the ordeal I had to withstand to purchase it. Yet nothing stopped me: not mouse-eaten parchments pulled out of raggedy parcels by old ladies who claimed succession rights based on having looked after a sick woman, or washed a corpse, or having given a half-basket of nuts during a year of famine; nor lying notaries or corrupt lawyers; nor afternoons spent in stuffy courtrooms, threats by building speculators, or unfavorable verdicts; not even sick children used as blackmail weapons. Not to mention émigrés now living in Spain who wanted to profit from the crazy infidel (me), and greedy intermediaries, and some dear friends who stabbed me in the back. Paradoxically, throughout ten years of legal battles I never doubted that my antagonists were acting in good faith, even when they cheated me and lied to me. They were convinced that this land really belonged to their ancestors who had broken their backs to squeeze a living from it, that it belonged to their cattle, to the sacred eagles that flew over it, to the warriors who had conquered it by killing their neighbors and raping their women. Poor peasants! How could they have known that I had been here a long, long time before them? The Gharsa Baqqali has been mine since forever.

The Gharsa Baqqali takes me out of myself and helps me rediscover myself again. In these fields, among fig trees planted one hundred years ago, I no longer can be a man who makes a garden. The very idea of a garden upsets me; I shake it off, like a mule does with horseflies. This is a place, and a place is much more than a garden. This is where you lie down to eat, sleep, study, think, pray, and make love. Sure, planting potatoes and onions in good soil is fine, or planting fruit trees so apricots can be picked in the spring and peaches in the summer. Sure, it is a duty to transplant the millions of bulbs that in this short-sighted country would be inevitably destroyed, like the trees and bushes already uprooted by murderous bulldozers. Yet, if for a single moment I were to become *aesthetic* and to conceive, God forbid, an image of nature subdued and refined, one of those images by which gardeners are so often blinded, then I would deserve to lose this wide piece of land. The *jennun*, the genies of this place, would become furious and hand it over to my adversaries. There is no difference between making pretty blossoming flowerbeds and rows of gray high-rise buildings.

Like the few beautiful places in northern Morocco that have been spared the destructive fury and stupidity of man, the Gharsa Baqqali is home to countless creatures: crickets, scorpions, dung beetles, snails, slugs, blindworms, herculean grass snakes, vipers, mice of all sorts, moles, hedgehogs, badgers, weasels, ferrets, and hares. The birds are so numerous that if they were to take off all together at the same time, they would blot out the sun. On these light-drenched slopes I replanted sage, irises, cat's head rockroses (*Helianthemum caput-felis*), shrubby hare's ears (*Bupleurum fruticosum*), daffodils, meadow saffron (*Colchicum autumnale*), crocuses, romuleas, merenderas, scillas, and tassel hyacinths (*Muscari comosum*). In the level ground I

planted gladioli and umbellifers; oleanders and chasteberries where the earth is moist; cork oaks and mastic trees where shade is required; young fig trees among the old ones (in northern Morocco alone there are more than 150 varieties of fig trees, each of them with its own name). Driven by my passion and guided by the *jennun*, I have accomplished all this. As I said, there is no place for "pretty" here, but only for the melancholic splendor of this valley over the sea. The rule is simple and strict: only indigenous plants can be introduced here. It's forbidden to foreigners, even if they have been part of the landscape for centuries. Not even Mexican prickly pears are allowed in these fields. And no buildings, except the reed hut that has become our school. However, my office is right here; it is the shade of an ancient wild olive tree. When I am in the Gharsa Baqqali I don't feel the need to escape from myself, or from my gardens, to go to some place I haven't yet been. I do not need to leave the room, be it of stone or greenery — I am already outside! And when I am lying between the daffodils, eating *tajine* in the company of my beloved gardeners and their little sisters, I realize how lovely it is to be together. I remember long ago when we were pirates, gathered all together in this clearing, laughing and tossing the doubloons of our booty into the air; I even recall an earlier time when with flint knives, our mouths watering with anticipation, we butchered the boar we'd just killed with our spears. For such a long time have I been in my beloved Gharsa Baqqali that I no longer know where I leave off and it begins, where its trees finish and my arms commence, where is the sorrow and where the birds, whose are the thoughts and whose the breath.

PAGES 186–187: Ngoc's fig tree with a view of the sea in the background. She claims that a photograph of this tree taken on her first trip to Rohuna is her self-portrait — *Ficus carica* 'Ngoc Minh Ngo'.

PAGE 189: The *Glebionis segetum* are at the end of their blooming. Summer is coming.

OPPOSITE: *Narcissus papyraceus* under the fig trees. Every year we plant thousands of these narcissi, rescuing them from the construction sites of buildings and roads.

PAGES 192–193: Fava beans in the fig orchard in early March.

PAGES 194–195: A field of *Gladiolus communis* before the fig trees. On the horizon, the Phoenician hills overlooking the ocean.

PAGE 196: My office under a wild olive tree. The picture is taken from the new path traced by Hisham, which cuts through the wood.

PAGE 197: An August evening under the apricot tree.

OPPOSITE: Damask hybrid and centifolia roses, the old perfumed roses of northern Morocco.

PAGES 200–201: A small pipe of *kif* and a cup of mint tea are the best companions on a late summer afternoon.

PAGES 202-203: The third year of our orchard, which is planted with old local varieties of fruit trees.

PAGES 204-205: Summer light in the orchard at dusk.

OPPOSITE: All the non-indigenous flowers cultivated in the Gharsa Baqqali are used as cut flowers for the house, with the exception of the white lilies. It takes a long time for a seedling to become a floriferous bulb, and cutting the flowers weakens the bulbs, which prevents them from producing more blooms. They are part of the history and culture of Tangier, since they come from a region near Tangier called Anjra, where they have naturalized. The old peasant women who have cultivated them in their gardens for centuries are proud and jealous of their lilies, and to have a few bulbs I had to beg them on my knees.

WILD FLOWERS OF NORTHERN MOROCCO

I love the wild flowers of northern Morocco. This garden was created for them. It is my duty to save as many of them as possible. This duty is my pain and my pleasure.

Bulbous wild plants are seldom allowed in gardens. The bulbs flower for a short time. During the long period of rest they need to regenerate, the earth remains bare. Of course, if you really can't do without them, you can always put them in a pot. It is like owning a leopard and keeping it on a leash or having a monkey in the closet: a pointless cruelty.

Anyone who is willing to take a long and tiresome trip just to admire the blossoming of wild peonies that turns a wood of hazels into a fairy's ballroom should refrain from removing a flower from the place where it blooms — it is an act against nature. In years of traveling through Italy, France, Spain, and Greece, I have suffered for the disappearance of cyclamens, narcissi, violets, and other flowers that opened my eyes to the defenseless beauty of the world when I was a child. Here in northern Morocco I realized I could go on dreaming the dream of that little boy. It was a field of blue irises that was dotted, like a Byzantine tapestry, with the carnelians of pot marigolds, the tourmalines of ferulas, and the rubies of pheasant's eyes. Even if there is less biodiversity than in countries like Spain or Turkey, the concentration of botanical species in the Tangier region was astounding.

Twenty years ago the dream turned into a nightmare. Bulldozers and Caterpillars began to gut our forests, the lily-covered Atlantic dunes disappeared, and the sand was stolen to be mixed into cement. Apartment buildings, tourist marinas, and superstores popped up everywhere. I returned to the fields where I had known happiness. Between the new buildings of hatefulness I saw bulbs emerging from the devastated ground, which was strewn with plastic bags and filthy with cement. Among piles of rusting scrap metal and broken glass, uprooted trees and shrubs dried out like brushwood in the sun. I had to do something. Chance or destiny had brought me to Rohuna, to this rocky patch of land that could be reached only by walking for miles. I would transform it into a Noah's Ark for rescuing species threatened by extinction.

With the help of some young men from the village, I began to rescue plants from construction sites, clumping soil onto their roots and pruning them severely to enable them to grow again later. I remember the first time: I heard the weeping of the strawberry tree that had been mutilated by my shears. Even today, twenty years later, when the pick runs through the earth to spud out the roots, I feel as if it were running through my flesh. I waver, I take a deep breath, I think about the garden, and then I begin again. Meanwhile, I talk to the plant; I tell it I will take it to a safe place where it will be respected and treated with love, fertilized by a bee or butterfly, and live in peace among its sisters.

This is our mission: hundred-year-old olive trees lying like beached whales alongside the new superhighway; carob trees, seven species of rockrose, three of broom; hundreds of the strawberry trees so dear to the Jebalas (the *buchannu* occurs in fables, rhymes, and lullabies); viburnums, clematis, sages, orchids, oleander, and chasteberry trees which used to grow along the banks of streams that have been cemented over or diverted to irrigate golf courses or polo grounds. And bulbs, thousands, hundreds of thousands of bulbs. The Moroccan irises are bulbous, belonging to the subgenus *Xiphium*, except one. They all lived in this region. Between December and March the plain of

PAGES 208–209: A field of gladioli, a plant that normally flowers in cultivated fields. In January, we plough the earth lightly to disturb the corms, which makes them flower more abundantly.

PAGE 211: *Iris tingitana*, the iris of Tangier that once grew wild all over its native city, carpeting immense fields from the southwest to the east from December until March, has become a rare sight.

OPPOSITE: *Iris filifolia*, for me the most heraldic of the Moroccan irises.

PAGES 214 & 215: *Gladiolus communis* subsp. *byzantinus* and *Gladiolus communis* subsp. *communis*. One of the differences between these two subspecies is that all the flowers of the former have the same orientation, while those of the latter diverge. The former, with deep magenta flowers and stems as high as three feet, is a lone warrior that does not love to be near others and often grows between the thorny leaves of dwarf palms. The smaller and paler field gladiolus is a sociable peasant: it lives in large groups and loves to be caressed by the plough.

Tangier was entirely covered in *Iris tingitana*. Nobody who has witnessed this miracle will ever be able to forget it. It was like leaving reality behind, entering myth, wandering there, freely and happily. Today those flowers have almost disappeared, yet there is a valley where the miracle is renewed every year: our garden. From the Rif we have managed to save the *Iris serotina*, and from the clayey plains of the Beni Arros the *Iris fontanesii*. We saved hundreds of *Iris filifolia* that stood in purple splendor where the superhighway to Casablanca was built, as well as the last specimens of the rarest indigenous iris, the *Iris juncea* var. *numidica*, a small flower, yellow like the eyes of a panther. I begged the bulldozer drivers who were engaged in widening the road between Tangier and Cape Spartel to give me time to run home and get my pick and shovel. I had searched high and low without suspecting that it blossomed so late, in the middle of June, right alongside a road where I drove almost every day.

On the Loukkos estuary, a few miles north of Larache, lay an immense colony of *Iris planifolia*. Every autumn, acres of undergrowth became as blue as the sky with those large flowers that look like they have been put down on the ground. It was destroyed. In its place they built a marina, complete with villas, hotels, and the umpteenth golf course. And yet, the very mosquitoes that tormented us during our transplantation efforts (despite insect repellent and cortisone we were swollen and feverish for weeks) caused the marina to fail. It is empty now. Uninhabited. Thou blessed anopheles! To you and to your itch-injecting proboscis, I dedicate our field of *Iris planifolia* where the windy November sky can still behold itself.

We have brought here hundreds of sacks full of narcissus bulbs (*Narcissus papyraceus*, *N. serotinus*, *N. elegans*, *N. viridiflorus*, *N. tazetta*, *N. bulbocodium*, *N. cavanillesii*) — on our shoulders, on the backs of mules, by Jeep, and by tractor. We have brought gladioli (*Gladiolus communis*, *G. byzantinus*), ornithogalums (*Ornithogalum arabicum*, *O. collinum*, *O. unifolium*), alliums, crocuses, meadow saffron, scillas, dipcadis, romuleas, *Acis autumnalis*, and *A. tingitana*. Each of them has been replanted in the most suitable location because luckily we have all types of soil in our garden, ranging from acidic to alkaline, from fine-grained sand to pottery clay — although the latter is practically inert, many types of bulbs love it. Phoenician flowers, Roman flowers, Idrisid flowers, Almoravid flowers, Jebala flowers... Our garden is the refuge of all these fabulous creatures that have guarded the spirit of their land for hundreds of centuries. This is something that the local authorities responsible for the ecological disaster don't understand. But my young men do. These sons of peasants and shepherds, who have worked so hard with me to transplant these plants, trees, and flowers, they know it. And so do their sons, children of a humiliated Morocco that still is the most vital part of the country. The garden of Rohuna was created for the flowers. And the flowers are happy when children look at them.

OPPOSITE: Our collection of narcissi. Top row from left to right: *Narcissus elegans,* whose flat leaves come out at the same time as the flowers, which are in umbels of up to seven; *Narcissus cavanillesii,* found recently, the oldest of the Moroccan narcissi, a tiny creature with a non-existent corona and a gold corolla. I always imagined that during a hunt toward the end of the Paleolithic a little girl was killed by the tusks of a wounded mammoth. Her mother laid her down deep inside the cave, painted her body with red ochre, and encircled her forehead with a coronet of this narcissus. I see in this gesture the beginning of our civilization; *Narcissus viridiflorus.* Second row: *Narcissus tazetta; N. italicus; N. jonquilla.* Bottom row: *Narcissus papyraceus; N. bulbocodium; N.* 'Telamonius plenus', a seventeenth-century hybrid collected by John Tradescant and naturalized in the mountains around Rohuna. Likely they are descendants of the few bulbs given at the beginning of the twentieth century by the journalist Walter Harris, a Tangier correspondent for *The Times*, to his kidnapper and close friend Moulay Ahmed er Raisuni, the great outlaw who inspired the film *The Wind and the Lion*.

PAGES 218–219: The ancient warriors from the Jebala are finally saved — *Iris tingitana*, all transplanted from construction sites in and around Tangier, wave their feather caps and brandish their silver swords on the hillside.

OPPOSITE: *Dipcadi serotinum* — sometimes known as the brown bluebell — prefers rocky, stony, or sandy soil.

PAGE 222: *Narcissus elegans* blooming around an old olive tree transplanted several years ago. In the background, the hill looks as if it was painted by Giotto. I call it the "Phoenician hill" because it recalls ancient idylls, mysterious Chthonic cults.

PAGE 223: *Iris planifolia* saved from a construction site near a marina for tourists. They bloom in abundance every autumn in the Gharsa Baqqali.

OPPOSITE: Top row from left to right: *Acis autumnalis,* with its minuscule white flower that looks like a bell to summon fairies; *Allium nigrum; Gynandriris sisyrinchium,* whose fleeting flowers often don't open until late in the afternoon and wither the same evening. Second row: *Hyacinthoides lingulata,* with a scent comparable to the English bluebells, grows in abundance in short grass and cultivated fields; *Scilla peruviana,* which, despite its species name given by Linnaeus in 1753, is strictly a native of the Mediterranean region of Italy and Spain and North Africa; *Crocus serotinus* subsp. *salzmannii.* Bottom row: *Bellevalia dubia,* an early spring bloomer; *Prospero autumnale; Tulipa sylvestris.*

THE TRUE GARDEN

This story began twelve years ago. And twelve years old was Najim on the evening his mother gave him to me as a gift. The last of four boys and four girls, Najim was a rascal. Poor Mina was at a total loss with him. I had always been fond of him; our friend Sarah had a weakness for him too. But when Mina left her present in my kitchen, a rather complicated period began. I never wanted to have children, and it was not easy to find a school in Tangier prepared to accept our almost illiterate shepherd boy. The only one was an association dedicated to street children — it was presided over by an acquaintance of mine. The pupils not only studied, but also learned a trade. Najim chose to become a carpenter. After four endless years he obtained his diploma. We set up a company called "N.O.W. on the Ocean," (the acronym stands for "Najim's Own Workshop"). Inspired by two eighteenth-century "rustic" English chairs in the living room of my friend Christopher Gibbs (the first client and benefactor of N.O.W.), I designed some prototypes: benches, seats, large tables, small tables. It was Najim's task to build them, using arbutus branches that had to keep their natural form. We gave a party in Tangier to present them to the expatriate community. It was a success.

Najim has come back to live in Rohuna. His business is going well. But there are many others in our village who, like him, need help and encouragement. The world I knew during my first years here has vanished. Gone forever are the cold nights where we all huddled together in a room, while the wind made the zinc roof squeak and creak. This is when I understood what it is to be a man among other men. When electricity, television, and the road arrived, the *jennun* sought refuge in our garden. The Jebalan Arcadia has vanished. But a little bit of it still survives, right here, beneath the fig trees.

It is from here, from this garden, that I want to draw the economic resources and creative energy that will enable my young neighbors to live a better life. Nowadays, they can no longer be shepherds. The choice is between becoming a bricklayer's assistant in a nearby town or a kitchen help in a tourist restaurant. Stephan and I have decided to open the garden to the public. Part of the proceeds will go towards buying a cow and two sheep for the families and households in Rohuna that live below the poverty line. Then we will pave the stretch that runs between the houses, because the dust raised by cars is bad for health. The removal and sorting out of the trash need to be organized, and a *hammam*, a public bath, must be built.

Schooling is an urgent issue, especially for girls. I have reopened our little school in the Gharsa Baqqali hut. Twice a week a man from the Rif region comes to teach lessons in French, arithmetic, and geography to the gardeners and anyone else who wishes to attend. I have asked the old women of the village to teach their grand-daughters how to make the toys they played with fifty years ago, before the start of industrial toy-making. This is how the *arusa* have been born again — they are little reed-and-cloth bride dolls made by Soukeina, Fatima Zorah, Soraya, and Amina. They have been on display in galleries in Tangier, Madrid, London, and Milan. Part of the proceeds goes to the families so they can afford to buy books, school bags, and warm clothing for the little girls, since the local authorities have finally provided a school bus available to take them to the nearest school, which is three miles away — the rest goes into the future projects fund. The same goes for the mud-and-straw figures fired in a bread oven by Latifa and other girls, and for the animals of "Straw Zoo", a fabulous bestiary created with dwarf palm fibers by two cousins, Smail and Mohammed. Part goes to the young artists, part goes into the common pot.

I have been so lucky to enjoy the rare privilege of turning a stony ground into a garden. Although a foreigner, an infidel, an incompetent, one who has arrived here purely by coincidence, I have been helped and accepted by the dwellers of this remote village. Yet, if I reach out my hand it is not out of gratitude but out of love. My love for you, dear neighbors, who are my constant pain and joy, has taught me that a garden is not merely a space dedicated to the cultivation of plants; it is, above all, a place where men, women, children, and animals live in search of harmony, between each other and with the spirits of the earth. To become freer, we have to give ourself up to the mystery that surrounds us. In my dreams, Rohuna is this. Dig in, Chinioui! Dig in, Nabil, Lotfi, Hamidou! Don't go away. Study and learn to name the names of all your plants to foreigners! A little more effort and if the *jennun* are willing, one day we are going to make the true garden come true. (*They* are laughing out green: yes, they *are* willing.)

ABOVE: Sarah Rose in all her splendor. **RIGHT:** Bernard and me under a fig tree in the Gharsa Baqqali. **LOWER RIGHT:** Stephan in front of the oleanders; me among the gladioli; Ngoc in a rare moment before the camera.

LEFT: Jelel and Nabia and their daughters Soraya and Marwa. Elias, their boy, was no doubt playing soccer at the time. **LOWER LEFT:** The bridge that Najim gave us, and its author. **BELOW:** Bernard, known as "*Beljiki*".

PAGES 226–227: A palm tree was born next to a small olive tree, and the carob tree was too close to its brothers. After a week of rain, we are going to transplant them next to the stream that runs on the bottom of the valley of the *Iris tingitana*. I can't imagine a better way to start the day.

RIGHT: Mohammed, known as Chinioui, and his brother Lotfi. They have been my friends since they were born. And today they are the youngest gardeners.

LEFT: From top to bottom: Nabil, a great gardener; Amin, known as "Couman", the night guardian who also ploughs the land to sow potatoes, onions, garlic, fava, and other beans; Abdelhamid, the head gardener, a generous, gentle, and diligent man who is dedicated to his work. **BELOW:** Hisham, who takes marvelous care of the Gharsa Baqqali.

LEFT: The dolls team and their work: from left, Amina Imran "Costa", Myriam Imran, little Maha with her mother Soukeina Imran "Bando", Soraya Gharabi; in the back, Nadia Bouhajel and Assia Imran "Costa".

ABOVE: Mohammed and Ibrahim G'bari — the creators of "Straw Zoo" — and some of their animals and mythical characters, made by weaving the fiber of *doum*, the dwarf palm: the elephant, the Native American warriors, the hero/god on a chariot.

PAGES 232–233: It's a late summer afternoon. The tide is low, and a game of soccer is still being played on the beach. Not all of us are there, but nearly all, so this is our official photo. From left: Bernard Dogimont, Hamid Kribish, Cosimo Sesti, Amin "Couman" Imran "Bando" and his son Mohammed, Soraya Gharabi, Amina Imran "Costa", Sarah Rose Wheeler, Soukeina Imran "Bando" with her daughter Maha in her arm, Najim Imran "Bando", Fatima Zorah Imran, me, Ibrahim G'bari, Nabil Kribish, Abdelhak Tribak, Adbelhamid Imran, Abdelmajid "Mjiddo" Baqqali, Tarek Baqqali, Mohammed "Stituo" Imran, Jelel Gharabi with Marwa, Mohammed G'bari, Adam Imran, Mounir Imran and Aitam Gharabi in front of Stephan Janson, and (seated on his heels) Yassine Gharabi. The two dogs are the sisters Adèle (the brown-haired one) and Talitha (the black-and-white one). We all have a role in the life of the garden.

PLANT LIST

A
Acacia floribunda
Acacia karroo
Acacia mearnsii
Acacia podalyriifolia
Acacia saligna
Acanthus eminens
Acanthus mollis
Acca sellowiana
Acis autumnalis
Acis tingitana
Aechmea fasciata 'Variegata'
Aeonium arboreum
Aeonium arboreum 'Schwarzkopf'
Aeonium haworthii
Agapanthus umbellatus
Agave americana
Agave americana 'Marginata'
Agave attenuata
Agave bracteosa
Agave geminiflora
Agave guiengola
Agave havardiana
Agave sisalana
Agave victoriae-reginae
Agave vilmoriniana
Aglaomorpha coronans
Ajania pacifica
Alcea rosea
Allagoptera arenaria
Allium ampeloprasum
Allium massaessylum
Allium nigrum
Allium paniculatum subsp. *antiatlanticum*
Allium roseum
Allium triquetrum
Aloe arborescens
Aloe brevifolia (2 forms)
Aloe chabaudii
Aloe distans
Aloe divaricata
Aloe ferox
Aloe humilis
Aloe maculata
Aloe marlothii
Aloe mitriformis
Aloe peglerae
Aloe saponaria
Aloe suprafoliata
Aloe thraskii
Aloe tomentosa
Aloe vera
Aloe 'Hercules'
Aloiampelos ciliaris
Aloidendron barberae
Aloysia triphylla
Alyogyne hakeifolia
Amaryllis belladonna

Ammi visnaga
Anchusa azurea
Andryala integrifolia
Anisacanthus wrightii
Annona cherimola
Anredera cordifolia
Antigonon leptopus
Arbutus 'Marina'
Arbutus unedo
Arbutus unedo var. *rubra*
Arbutus x andrachnoides
Arbutus x androsterilis
Archontophoenix alexandrae
Arctotis hybrids
Argyranthemum frutescens
Argyratum frutescens hybrids
Arisarum vulgare
Aristolochia baetica
Artemesia herba-alba
Arundo donax
Arundo donax 'Variegata'
Asparagus albus
Asparagus densiflorus
Asparagus densiflorus 'Sprengeri'
Asparagus falcatus
Asparagus macowanii
Asparagus plumosus
Asparagus plumosus var. *cupressoides*
Asparagus virgatus
Asphodelus albus
Aspidistra elatior
Atriplex halimus
Atriplex undulata
Austrocylindropuntia subulata

B
Babiana stricta
Barleria albostellata
Bauhinia bowkeri
Bauhinia divaricata
Bauhinia galpinii
Bauhinia tomentosa
Bellevalia dubia
Bidens heterophylla
Bignonia capreolata
Billbergia sp.
Bombax ceiba
Boophone disticha
Borago officinalis
Brachychiton acerifolius
Brachychiton bidwillii
Brachychiton rupestris
Brahea armata
Brasiliopuntia brasiliensis
Brillantaisia subulugurica
Buddleja glomerata
Buddleja lindleyana
Buddleja madagascariensis

Buddleja saligna
Buddleja salvifolia
Bulbine frutescens 'Hallmark'
Bulbine latifolia
Bupleurum fruticosum

C
Caesalpina gilliesii
Calamintha nepeta
Calendula arvensis
Calliandra portoricensis
Calicotome spinosa
Campsis 'Summer Jazz Fire'
Campsis grandiflora
Campsis x tagliabuana 'Madame Galen'
Canna 'Bengal Tiger'
Canna 'Firebird'
Canna 'Phasion'
Canna 'Wyoming'
Canna edulis
Canna glauca 'Erebus'
Canna hybrids
Caralluma europaea
Carissa grandiflora
Carissa spinosa
Casimiroa edulis
Cassia candolleana
Cassia mexicana
Cassia spectabilis
Ceiba insignis
Ceiba speciosa
Centaurea pullata
Centaurium umbellatum
Ceratonia siliqua
Cercis siliquastrum
Cereus aethiops
Cereus hildmannianus
Cerinthe major 'Purpurascens'
Cerinthe minor
Cestrum aurantiacum
Cestrum nocturnum
Cestrum parqui
Chamaedorea elegans
Chamaerops cerifera
Chamaerops humilis
Chasmanthe floribunda
Chilopsis linearis
Chitalpa x tashkentensis
Chlorophytum comosum
Chlorophytum comosum 'Variegata'
Chrysanthemum carinatum
Cichorium intybus
Cinnamomum camphora
Cistus albidus
Cistus atriplicifolium
Cistus clusii
Cistus crispus
Cistus halimifolius

Cistus halimifolius 'Cap Sim'
Cistus ladanifer
Cistus libanotis
Cistus monspeliensis
Cistus ocymoides
Cistus populifolius
Cistus pulverulentus
Cistus salviifolius
Cistus x aguilarii 'Maculatus'
Cistus x purpureus
Cistus x skanbergii
Citharexylum spicatum
Citharexylum spinosum
Citrus aurantium
Citrus aurantium 'Mirtifolia'
Citrus limequat
Citrus limon
Citrus reticulata
Cleistocactus strausii
Clematis cirrhosa
Clematis flammula
Clivia miniata
Clivia miniata 'Lutea'
Coccoloba uvifera
Colchicum autumnale
Colchicum longifolium
Coleus forskohlii hybrids
Colvillea racemosa
Convolvulus althaeoides
Convolvulus sabatius
Convolvulus tricolor
Cordia boissieri
Cordia lutea
Cordyline australis
Cordyline fruticosa cultivar
Cordyline stricta
Coronilla valentina
Cortaderia selloana
Cotyledon macrantha
Cotyledon orbiculata
Cotyledon orbiculata 'Elk Horn'
Cotyledon tomentosa
Crassula arborescens
Crassula arborescens 'Undulata'
Crassula multicava
Crassula ovata 'Gollum'
Crataegus monogyna
Crinum amabile
Crinum moorei
Crinum moorei 'Album'
Crinum pedunculatum
Crinum x powellii
Crinum x powellii 'Album'
Crocus serotinus subsp. *salzmannii*
Crotalaria agatiflora
Cupressus sempervirens
Cupressus sempervirens 'Fastigiata'
Cussonia paniculata subsp. *sinuata*
Cussonia sphaerocephala
Cyclamen cilicium
Cyclamen hederifolium
Cyclamen mirabile
Cyclamen rhodium
Cydonia oblonga
Cymbopogon citratus
Cynara cardunculus

Cytisus linifolius

D

Dahlia imperialis
Daphne gnidium
Dasylirion serratifolium
Datura metel hybrids
Daucus carota
Delairea odorata
Delonix regia
Delosperma kofleri
Dianthus caryophyllus hybrids
Dichrostachys cinerea
Dicliptera suberecta
Dietes bicolor
Dietes grandiflora
Diospyros kaki
Dipcadi serotinum
Dodonea viscosa
Dombeya rotundifolia
Dombeya tiliacea
Dracaena deremensis 'Variegata'
Dracaena draco
Duranta erecta 'Geisha Girl'
Duranta excelsa

E

Echinocactus grusonii
Echium fastuosum
Echium vulgare
Elaeagnus x ebbingei
Emilia javanica
Encephalartos ferox
Epiphyllum oxypetalum
Eremophila maculata
Eremophila maculata yellow form
Eremophila maculata orange form
Erica arborea
Eriobotrya deflexa
Eriobotrya japonica
Eriocephalus africanus
Erysimum linifolium
Erythrina crista-galli
Erythrina herbacea
Erythrina humeana
Erythrina vespertilio
Erythrina x bidwillii
Eschscholzia californica
Eucalyptus camaldulensis
Eucalyptus kruseana
Euphorbia canariensis
Euphorbia candelabrum
Euphorbia ceratocarpa
Euphorbia characias
Euphorbia characias subsp. *wulfenii*
Euphorbia cotinifolia
Euphorbia dendroides
Euphorbia enterophora
Euphorbia grandidens
Euphorbia ingens
Euphorbia milii hybrid
Euphorbia officinarum
Euphorbia regis-jubae
Euphorbia resinifera
Euphorbia rigida
Euphorbia segetalis

Euphorbia stenoclada
Euphorbia tirucalli
Euphorbia xanti
Euryops chrysanthemoides
Euryops pectinatus
Euryops virgineus

F

Felicia amelloides
Felicia echinata
Ficus carica
Ficus cyathistipula
Ficus lutea
Ficus sycomorus
Foeniculum vulgare 'Bronze'
Fouquieria splendens
Freesia alba
Fremontodendron californicum
Furcraea foetida
Furcraea macdougalii

G

Galactites tomentosa
Gardenia jasminoides
Gardenia jasminoides 'Kleim's Hardy'
Gardenia thunbergia
Gardenia volkensii
Gaura lindheimeri 'Siskiyou Pink'
Gazania rigens hybrids
Geranium canariense
Geranium pratense
Gladiolus communis subsp. *byzantinus*
Gladiolus communis subsp. *communis*
Gladiolus tristis
Glebionis coronaria
Glebionis segetum
Glottiphyllum longum
Gonialoe variegata
Greyia radlkoferi
Gynandriris sisyrinchium

H

Haemanthus coccineus
Hakea laurina
Hamelia patens
Harpephyllum caffrum
Hedera helix
Helianthemum caput-felis
Helianthus annuus
Helichrysum italicum
Helichrysum petiolare
Hemerocallis hybrids
Hesperaloe funifera
Hesperaloe parviflora
Hibiscus cannabinus
Hibiscus coccineus
Hibiscus syriacus hybrids
Hibiscus tiliaceus
Hibiscus mutabilis
Hippeastrum hybrids
Holmskioldia sanguinea
Homalocladium platycladum
Howea forsteriana
Hyacinthoides lingulata
Hylocereus undatus
Hymenosporum flavum

Hypoestes aristata

I

Ipomoea arborescens
Ipomoea learii
Iresine herbstii
Iris filifolia
Iris foetidissima
Iris fontanesii
Iris germanica
Iris germanica var. *florentina*
Iris juncea var. *numidica*
Iris orientalis
Iris planifolia
Iris planifolia 'Alba'
Iris pseudacorus
Iris serotina
Iris tingitana
Iris unguicularis
Iris xiphion hybrids

J

Jacaranda mimosifolia
Jacobaea maritima
Jasminum grandiflorum
Jasminum multipartitum
Jasminum odoratissimum
Jasminum polyanthum
Jasminum sambac 'Grand Duke of Tuscany'
Jatropha gossypifolia
Jatropha integerrima
Jatropha multifida
Justicia spicigera

K

Kalanchoe beharensis
Kalanchoe beharensis 'Fang'
Kalanchoe beharensis 'Maltese Cross'
Kalanchoe blossfeldiana
Kalanchoe daigremontiana
Kalanchoe fedtschenkoi
Kalanchoe humilis
Kalanchoe laetivirens
Kalanchoe marmorata
Kalanchoe marnieriana
Kalanchoe thyrsiflora
Kalanchoe tomentosa
Kleinia anteuphorbium
Kleinia mandraliscae
Kleinia neriifolia
Koelreuteria elegans
Kumara plicatilis
Kundmannia sicula

L

Lantana camara hybrids
Lathyrus odoratus
Laurus nobilis
Lavandula dentata
Lavandula stoechas
Lavandula x intermedia
Lavatera trimestris
Lavatera arborea
Leonotis leonurus
Leucaena leucocephala
Leucophyllum frutescens

Ligustrum lucidum
Lilium candidum
Lilium longiflorum
Limonium latifolium
Liriope muscari
Lobelia excelsa
Lobelia tupa
Lomandra hystrix
Lonicera japonica
Lophocereus marginatus
Lotus corniculatus
Loxostylis alata
Lycianthes rantonnetii
Lycium intricatum
Lygos sphaerocarpa

M

Mackaya bella
Malope trifida
Mandragora officinarum
Mangifera indica
Manihot esculenta
Markhamia lutea
Matthiola incana 'Alba'
Melia azedarach
Melianthus comosus
Melianthus major
Mentha spicata
Mentha pulegium
Mentha rotundifolia
Merendera filifolia
Metrosideros excelsa
Mirabilis jalapa hybrids
Montanoa bipinnatifida
Montanoa hibiscifolia
Montanoa tomentosa
Moringa hildebrandtii
Moringa oleifera
Morus alba
Morus nigra
Muehlenbeckia complexa
Muscari comosum
Myoporum laetum
Myrsine africana
Myrtus communis
Myrtus communis 'Boetica'
Myrtus communis 'Tarentina'

N

Narcissus 'Telamonius plenus'
Narcissus 'Tête-à-tête'
Narcissus broussonetii
Narcissus bulbocodium
Narcissus cavanillesii
Narcissus elegans
Narcissus italicus
Narcissus jonquilla
Narcissus papyraceus
Narcissus serotinus
Narcissus tazetta
Narcissus viridiflorus
Nephrolepis cordifolia
Nerine bowdenii
Nerium oleander
Nerium oleander hybrids
Nicotiana mutabilis

Nolina nelsonii
Nonea pulla

O

Olea europea
Olea europea var. *oleaster*
Ophrys apifera
Opuntia aciculata
Opuntia gosseliniana
Opuntia microdasys
Opuntia robusta
Orbea variegata
Ornithogalum arabicum
Ornithogalum collinum
Ornithogalum dubium
Ornithogalum unifolium
Osteospermum hybrids

P

Papaver rhoeas
Papaver somniferum
Pavonia hastata
Pelargonium 'Nutmeg Scented'
Pelargonium capitatum 'True Rose'
Pelargonium denticulatum
Pelargonium grandiflorum hybrids
Pelargonium graveolens
Pelargonium peltatum hybrids
Pelargonium odoratissimum
Pelargonium quercifolium
Pelargonium sidoides
Pelargonium tomentosum
Pelargonium zonale
Pennisetum setaceum 'Rubrum'
Pericallis x hybrida
Philadelphus 'Sybille'
Phoenix canariensis
Phoenix dactylifera
Phormium tenax
Phyllirea angustifolia
Phyllirea latifolia
Phytolacca dioica
Pilosocereus sp.
Pinus halepensis
Pinus pinaster
Pinus pinea
Pistacia atlantica
Pistacia lentiscus
Pistacia terebinthus
Pittosporum brevicalyx
Pittosporum tobira
Pittosporum undulatum
Platanus x acerifolia
Plectranthus argentatus
Plectranthus lanceolatus
Plectranthus lanuginosus
Plectranthus neochilus
Plectranthus parvifolius
Plectranthus tomentosa
Plumbago capensis 'Dark Blue'
Podranea ricasoliana
Poinsettia pulcherrima
Populus sp.
Populus sp. 'Fastigiata'
Portulacaria afra
Prospero autumnale

Prunus armeniaca
Prunus domestica
Prunus dulcis
Prunus persica
Pseudobombax ellipticum 'Alba'
Pseudocydonia sinensis
Pseudogynoxys chenopodioides
Psidium guajava
Pteridium aquilinum
Punica granatum
Pyrostegia venusta
Pyrus mamorensis

Q
Quercus coccifera
Quercus ilex
Quercus suber
Quercus virginiana
Quisqualis indica

R
Reinwardtia indica
Rhamnus alaternus
Rhoicissus rhomboidea
Ridolfia segetum
Roldana petasitis
Romneya coulteri
Romulea bulbocodium
Romulea engleri
Romulea maroccana
Rosa 'Belle Portugaise'
Rosa 'Complicata'
Rosa 'Guinée'
Rosa 'La Follette'
Rosa 'Lorraine Lee'
Rosa 'Mermaid'
Rosa 'Mme Isaac Pereire'
Rosa 'Mutabilis'
Rosa 'Quatre Saisons'
Rosa 'Rose de Rescht'
Rosa 'Sanguinea'
Rosa banksiae 'Lutea'
Rosa canina
Rosa centifolia hybrids
Rosa gigantea
Rosa sempervirens
Rosa sericea f. *pteracantha*
Rosa x damascena hybrids
Rosa x fortuniana
Rosmarinus officinalis
Rosmarinus officinalis 'Prostratus'
Ruellia brittoniana compact form
Ruellia brittoniana pink form
Ruellia brittoniana white form
Ruellia humilis
Ruscus aculeatus
Ruscus hypophyllum
Russelia equisetiformis
Ruta graveolens
Ruttya fruticosa

S
Saccharum officinarum
Saccharum officinarum 'Purpurea'
Salvia barrelieri
Salvia canariensis
Salvia coccinea
Salvia coccinea pink form
Salvia farinacea
Salvia greggii
Salvia jamensis 'La Luna'
Salvia microphylla
Salvia officinalis
Salvia pratensis
Salvia uliginosa
Sansevieria cylindrica
Sansevieria roxburghiana
Sansevieria trifasciata
Sansevieria trifasciata 'Dwarf Laurentii'
Sansevieria trifasciata 'Laurentii'
Santolina chamaecyparissus
Schefflera arboricola
Schinus molle
Schinus terebinthifolius
Schotia brachypetala
Scilla mauritanica
Scilla monophyllos
Scilla obtusifolia
Scilla peruviana
Scolymus hispanicus
Sedum palmeri
Sedum reflexum
Selenicereus grandiflorus
Senecio tamoides
Serapias lingua
Smilax aspera
Solandra grandiflora
Solanum seaforthianum
Solanum sodomaeum
Sophora tomentosa
Sorgho bicolor
Spartium junceum
Spathodea campanulata
Spathodea campanulata 'Lutea'
Sphaeralcea ambigua
Sphaeralcea fendleri
Sprekelia formosissima
Stephanotis floribunda
Strelitzia juncea
Strelitzia nicolai
Strelitzia reginae
Strelitizia reginae 'Mandela's Gold'
Styphnolobium japonicum
Synadenium grantii
Synadenium grantii 'Rubra'

T
Tacinga palmadora
Tagetes lemmonii
Tagetes lucida
Tecoma castaneifolia
Tecoma fulva
Tecoma garrocha
Tecoma red hybrid
Tecoma stans
Tecoma x smithii
Tecomaria capensis
Tecomaria capensis hybrids
Tetradenia riparia
Teucrium fruticans
Teucrium fruticans 'Ouarzazate'
Teucrium marum
Thapsia garganica
Thevetia peruviana
Thevetia thevetioides
Thymus mastichina
Tillandsia bergeri
Tipuana tipu
Tithonia diversifolia
Tithonia rotundifolia
Tithonia rotundifolia hybrids
Torilis arvensis
Trachaelospermum asiaticum
Trachaelospermum jasminoides
Trachelium caeruleum
Tradescantia pallida
Tradescantia zebrina
Trichocereus pachanoi
Tropaeolum majus
Tulbaghia violacea
Tulipa sylvestris
Tylecodon paniculatus

U
Urginea maritima
Urginea undulata
Urospermum dalechampii

V
Vauquelinia californica
Verbascum sinuatum
Verbena bonariensis
Viburnum suspensum
Viburnum tinus
Vinca difformis
Vinca major 'Variegata'
Viola odorata
Vitex agnus-castus
Vitex rotundifolia
Vitex trifolia 'Purpurea'
Vitis vinifera

W
Warionia saharae
Washingtonia filifera
Watsonia vanderspuyiae
Withania frutescens

Y
Yucca aloifolia
Yucca desmetiana
Yucca elephantipes
Yucca rostrata

Z
Zamia furfuracea
Zantedeschia aethiopica
Zinnia hybrids
Zizyphus vulgaris

Ngoc Minh Ngo is a celebrated photographer and the author of two books, *Bringing Nature Home: Floral Arrangements Inspired by Nature*, and *In Bloom: Creating and Living with Flowers*, both published by Rizzoli.

Umberto Pasti is a well-known Italian writer and horticulturalist.

Martina Mondadori is the founder of *Cabana* magazine. In addition to overseeing the design and production of *Cabana*, Mondadori is the European editor-at-large for *Town & Country* magazine.

ACKNOWLEDGMENTS

We are grateful to the families, friends, gardeners, editors whose hard work, inspiration, and support have made this book possible. It is simply not possible here to name everyone. We want to thank Deborah Needleman, who introduced us and sowed the seed of this book; Madison Cox, who first nurtured it; Martina Mondadori, whose support made it bloom into publication; Davide Tortorella, who helped transplanting the garden onto these pages; and Teresa Cremisi and Beatrice Masini, who affectionately watered it.

Thank you to Matthew Axe for the elegant design that captures the beauty of Rohuna and to Angela Taormina for ensuring every detail of the book is in order.

Thank you to Charles Miers and his team at Rizzoli for turning the book into a delicious fruit.

FIRST PUBLISHED
in the United States of America in 2019 by
Rizzoli International Publications, Inc.
300 Park Avenue South, New York, NY 10010
www.rizzoliusa.com

Text © Umberto Pasti

Photographs & Illustrations © Ngoc Minh Ngo

Publisher: Charles Miers
Editor: Dung Ngo
Book Designer: Matthew Axe
Production Design: Angela Taormina
Production Manager: Kaija Markoe
Managing Editor: Lynn Scrabis

ALL RIGHTS RESERVED.
No part of this publication may be reproduced, stored in a retrieval system, or transmitted in any form or by any means, electronic, mechanical, photocopying, recording, or otherwise, without prior consent of the publishers.

PRINTED IN CHINA

2019 2020 2021 2022 / 10 9 8 7 6 5 4 3 2 1

ISBN: 978-0-8478-6480-5
Library of Congress Control Number: 2019933539

Visit us online:
Facebook.com/RizzoliNewYork
Twitter: @Rizzoli_Books
Instagram.com/RizzoliBooks
Pinterest.com/RizzoliBooks
Youtube.com/user/RizzoliNY
Issuu.com/Rizzoli